The AUSTRALIAN Women's Week

Colour
in your garden

By Angus Stewart & John Stowar

*Every garden can become an artist's palette, using nature as the medium.
Brighten the view of visitors to your garden with clever colour combinations and
inspiring plantings. This book covers a wide selection of garden styles, seasons and
climates to give you information, inspiration and ideas on how to create your own
piece of colourful paradise*

❖ ❖ ❖

A Vision Splendid

Add colour to your life

A garden filled with colour is one of the great rewards of getting your hands dirty. As the blooms unfurl and the leaves turn, even the most unwilling gardener gets a surge of pride and experiences a sense of wonder at the beauty of nature. Colour moves people. Sometimes it provides a sense of peace and tranquillity, sometimes excitement and drama. Its effect is always changing according to the time of day, the weather, the season, and your mood.

Don't be afraid of colour, even the brighter hues - learn to use it to your advantage. Create a spectacular living artwork in your backyard by using colourful plants in an imaginative way. There are few things more enchanting than beds and borders awash with colour, or a brightly painted arch or gate surrounded by flowers in complementary tones.

Colour can create a beautiful haven but it can just as easily become a demanding tyrant. Think about what you want to create, don't go overboard buying all the pots in flower at the nursery one week and then stand back to find that you have simply planted an unruly jungle. Colour needs careful orchestration.

On the following pages you'll find a range of inspirational ideas and practical information. There's advice on combining colour - what works well and why; introducing colour with leaves, bark and fruit as well as flowers, plus designs for a sunny blue garden, a white courtyard, a tropical retreat, a golden terrace and a formal pink garden.

The brightly coloured blooms of the harlequin flower (*Sparaxis 'tricolour'*) are an attention-grabber in any garden. Combined with the variegated foliage of Hebe 'Veronica' the effect is dramatic but not overwhelming.

Nothing evokes the feeling of spring more than beds filled with beautiful tulips. Pristine tulips underplanted with white pansies creates a statement of simple elegance. Standard roses complete the formal design.

A purple carpet has been created with a mass planting of Lobularia. These dainty rounded flowers also come in pink and white. Here they are flanked by the tall blooms of Anenomes in complementary shades of red and blue.

Many trees are awash with colour in autumn. The spreading branches of the deciduous tulip tree (*Liriodendron tulipifera*) turn from deep green to glorious yellow in autumn and tulip-shaped pale flowers appear in spring.

As well as adding brilliant colour to a garden, this mass of poppies will make fabulous cut flowers. Cutting poppies will also extend their flowering season.

4

Colour *by* Design

The seduction of colour

Colour plays such an important role in our lives. It affects our moods enormously – a burst of yellow is at once warming and cheering, a flush of red is vibrant and exciting, a mass of blue and mauve is soothing, and white is always refreshing.

Today, more thought is given to the colour schemes we use in our homes, our workplaces, in private and government institutions, and in our gardens. Many hospitals and health centres are now moving away from sterile white walls in favour of warming yellows in recovery wards and entrances, or cooling blues in emergency areas. Advertising agencies, too, know the lure of colour: green is used to assure us of a product's freshness, red and orange to stimulate our

interest. In corporate boardrooms, deep reds or blues are used to suggest authority and power.

Attractive Foliage

Plant nurseries have long realised the seduction of colour. If a plant is in glorious colour, the chances of a sale are much greater than if it's not in flower. As a result nurseries are rife with pots and pots of colourful seasonal blooms and all too often we buy plants based on their appearance giving no thought to blending them with the existing garden.

Bright flowers are eye-catching so they attract customers more readily than pastels. The same applies to foliage. Reds and burgundies, golds and creams and all forms of variegated foliage attract attention more than the diversity of greens. In autumn, especially in cooler climates where the spectacle of foliage colour change is most visible, exceptional coloured specimens almost walk out the door!

The Impact of Colour

Light determines the colours we see. Flower and foliage colours change daily as the sun moves, and as the light changes with the seasons so do the colours of the garden. Orange and yellow flowers are intensified in the morning sun while on an overcast day even the brightest of flowers are muted. Pale coloured flowers seem to glow at dusk while the deep red shades fade into the darkness. Canny real estate salespeople will always advise a return visit to a property on a sunny day if the first inspection happened to fall on a dull and dreary day – such is the persuasive power of sunshine.

The gardens which make an impact on us and linger in our memory are often the gardens in which colour is a big feature. Indeed, misguided though it may be, garden competition winners have routinely been those in which a riot of colour prevails. Fortunately most judges, and more and more gardeners, now appreciate that the home garden, if it is to be a well-designed peaceful haven, is not the place for a riot!

We need to look beyond gaudy colour combinations to the functions of garden spaces, plant shapes, foliage textures and the suitability of plants for specific situations. In short, good design depends on much more than just colour. It's practical as well as visual.

The glorious red foliage of Japanese maple (*Acer palmatum*) (1) adds a dramatic splash of colour in a garden corner. The violet baboon flower, (*Babiana stricta*), perfectly complements the paler forget-me-nots (*Myosotis*) (2). Pansies (*Viola x wittrockiana*) in shades of purple provide an effective contrast to white Chrysanthemum daisies (*Chrysanthemum paludosum*) (3).

The red and green foliage of a *Coleus blumei* successfully brightens a shady spot beneath a tree. A popular soft-wooded perennial, it grows quickly to fill in garden spaces.

L.Clapp

A subtle spring display mixes annuals such as pink pansies (*Viola x wittrockiana*) and forget-me-nots (*Myosotis*) with perennials including Aquilegia and scrambling roses, such as the white 'Cecile Brunner' and pink 'Raubritter'. The misty haze of early morning combined with the pastel colours gives the garden a delicate glow.

The Influence of Seasons, Weather and Time of Day

*B*e sensitive to the changing personality of your garden according to season, weather and time of day. Learn to recognise the way light can transform a garden at different times of day. With the soft, low light of early morning, glimmering late afternoon light, cloudy skies and misty haze, the garden takes on a subtle glow, while the harsh midday sun tends to intensify strong colours such as yellow and gold and bleach whites. But strong sun can have its place and in sculptural gardens where form is everything, with strong shadows accentuating the forms in bright sunshine in high summer.

Cool greys, blues, lilacs, pinks and pale yellow perform well in the morning sun. Forget-me-nots (Myosotis), Brachycomes, Agapanthus and crepe myrtles (Lagerstroemia indica) should be planted in easterly facing aspects to take full advantage of the early morning light, while low-angled late afternoon sun is effective for warm colours.

At twilight, dark, non-reflective colours (which recede at all times) actually disappear but pastels and whites (which appear closer to you), become brilliant. Increased humidity levels can also affect the garden, softening those colours which appear bright. One of life's simplest pleasures is to walk in a garden in a light rain or mist, enjoying the soft light and subtle colour which abounds.

A beautiful blend of plants combines to create a shrubby border with the silvery-grey foliage of lavender providing a perfect foil for the white 'Iceberg' roses and the pink 'La Reine Victoria' roses. The pastel colours are highlighted by the surrounding greenery and the crisp white of the house wall. Garden borders of this style can be used successfully to frame a pathway or draw attention to an architectural feature in a garden.

How We See Colours

Understanding the colour spectrum and how we see colours will help you to choose a pleasing colour scheme for your garden. A rainbow, created when sunlight passes through raindrops, displays the entire range of colours which the human eye can see – from short wavelength violet to long wavelength red. When all these colours are combined the result is white light.

Colour is actually reflected light which is modified by the pigment (or colour) of varying surfaces. The pigment absorbs some of the wavelengths (colours) of the light spectrum and reflects others, resulting in the colour we see.

Reflection is also influenced by textures or surface quality. Smooth, glossy, pitted, sticky or hairy surfaces will each reflect light differently. This is easy to see if you compare a piece of satin with a piece of velvet both dyed exactly the same colour. Because of its finer texture and shiny surface the satin reflects more light, so it appears to be much lighter than the velvet. For example, *Anthurium* has a satin texture while petunias have a velvet sheen, making petunia flowers look even darker.

Another example is polar bear hair which is not white but clear. We see it as white because the hair shafts contain tiny, white air bubbles which refract and reflect the sun's light. The same thing happens with some white flowers – the petals appear white because tiny air spaces in the plant's tissue cause the light to be scattered so the surface appears to be white.

The tulip tree (*Liriodendron tulipifera*) in all its autumn glory.

Walk on the Wild Side

The main reason why flowers and foliage are coloured is to attract pollinators, either insects or mammals. Colour guides pollinators to flowers and different flowers and colours are attractive to certain types of pollinators. Animals perceive colour in varying ways and diverse colours attract quite different groups of animals.

Birds have excellent colour perception in the red range so usually a red-flowered plant will be bird-pollinated. This is even more likely if the plant has a tubular flower which is rich in nectar as well. The tubular flower has adapted to accomodate the long bill that most nectar-feeding birds possess. So if you want to attract birds to your garden, be sure to include some of the varieties of this interesting group of plants with their showy, colourful flowers. Grevilleas are among the most popular examples of plants with tubular flowers with a couple of the best being the ever-blooming hybrids 'Robyn Gordon' and 'Superb'.

Many insects are attracted to the blue to yellow end of the colour spectrum. Insects such as iridescent jewel beetles and gaudy butterflies enticed by the flowers will fascinate children, and adults, for hours.

Tubular flowers such as Christmas bells (*Blandfordia*) (1) are ideal for attracting birds to your garden. Other favourites with birds include gum blossoms (*Eucalyptus caesia*) (2), kangaroo paws such as *Anigozanthos* 'Bush Ranger' (3), Grevillea 'Superb' (4) and the waratah (*Telopea speciosissima*) (5).

The Colour Wheel

S tudying the colour wheel will help you to understand colour qualities and their relationships and this in turn will strengthen your ability to create moods and pictures within a garden.

For many of us, experimenting with colour in our gardens may be the closest we ever get to painting, and we can learn from the way painters use and blend colour. A gardener, unlike a painter, cannot change the colours in a garden by mixing different pigments together but intriguing effects can none the less be created by clever colour combinations.

The colour wheel at right demonstrates which colours are complementary (those adjacent on the wheel) and contrasting (those opposite on the wheel). Primary hues, secondary hues and tertiary hues are indicated on the wheel.

● Primary hues are red, yellow and blue; they exist in their own right and are not made by mixing other colours.

● Secondary hues are orange, green and violet; they are created by combining two primary colours in equal amounts. For example; orange is made by mixing red and yellow, green is made by mixing yellow and blue, and violet is made by mixing red and blue.

● Tertiary hues are the result of combining primary and secondary colours - red and orange for scarlet, blue and green for turquoise and so on.

A hue, or pure colour, can be made darker by adding black so that a shade of that hue is created. The addition of white to the hue creates a tint, and the addition of grey produces a tone (also called the brightness).

Perfect Harmony

In all great works of art, one colour will usually dominate and this applies as much to a garden as it does to paintings or decorating. Colour harmony is an essential ingredient in producing a restful, successful garden design. By using varying shades of the one colour, adjacent to one another on the colour wheel, you will produce a balance of colour. For example, varieties of daffodils provide a glorious display of the diverse shades of yellow, ranging from buttery cream and pale lemon to vibrant yellow. In this simple form of colour harmony, the brightest colour should be used sparingly so it doesn't dominate overall.

Many gardeners like to use assorted shades of blue and mauve in their gardens as it creates a calming atmosphere. Hydrangeas, Agapanthus and Jacarandas, all wonderful summer-flowering plants, can be used to great effect in this way.

Perhaps a more adventurous option is to design a garden which combines three warm hues which lie next to one another on the colour wheel, such as yellow, orange and deep gold. The focal point is achieved by including the stronger, primary hue of yellow. Try painting an arbor or door in a deep shade of yellow, then surround it with a mass planting of golden marigolds and orange Californian poppies. Just brilliant! Paler, or more pastel, shades of yellow, perhaps some creamy yellow daffodils or Liliums, would be best used towards the periphery of the scene.

A dramatic effect is created with bold colour combinations such as these yellow, orange and red snapdragrons (*Antirrhinum*).

The glorious range of colours in marigolds (*Calendula*), above, are a classic example of monochromatic harmony – shades of the one colour are planted together to give a balance of colour. Vibrant 'Moonbeam' yellow marigolds are combined with the orange tones of 'Solar Gold'.

If you have a dry, sunny spot and want colour all year round, opt for the blooms of blanket flowers (*Gaillardia*) and yellow buttons *(Pseudognaphalium ramosissimum)*, above. Tuberous Begonias, below, provide a brilliant flush of colour in shades ranging from the palest dusky rose to fire engine red.

Changing Face of Flowers

ydrangeas are the most vivid illustration of how gardeners can alter flower colour but some flowers naturally change colour as they age. In such cases the flower pigments undergo chemical changes as they become older. The old favourite garden plant, Yesterday, Today and Tomorrow **(Brunfelsia bonodora)***, above, is one of the best examples of this as the flowers open with a deep violet colour which gradually fades to*

pale blue and finally to white over a period of three or so days. All three colours are represented on the bush at the same time. In other flowers, such as kangaroo paws, colour is heavily influenced by temperature. In this case the higher the temperature the lighter the flower will become, so that a variety such as **Anigozanthos 'Bush Ranger'***, which is normally bright red, can turn a pinkish colour under heatwave conditions.*

The blue blooms of forget-me-nots *(Myosotis)* **perfectly highlight the bright pink flowers of Silene, above.**

The brightly coloured flowers of *Babiana,* above, which are similar to freesias, are popular with many gardeners.
Don't overlook the appeal of herbs when choosing colourful plants for your garden. The tiny blue flowers of thyme make a pretty and fragrant groundcover, and when combined with the larger-petalled phlox, above, the effect is a beautiful sea of blue. Both do well in sun or semi-shaded positions.
Unusual colour combinations can be quite successful – the mauve tones of lavender sit comfortably with the crimson flowers of *Centranthus,* below.

Mass Appeal

Planting drifts of colour

Agapanthus

C olourful gardens always look more effective when plantings are massed in blocks or drifts of the same hue. This can be particularly striking when used along a driveway or entrance. A row of Agapanthus is a favourite with many gardeners – these hardy perennials offer lush green foliage year-round and provide the bonus of striking blue or white flowers in the summer. Another favourite is a line of deciduous trees which shade a driveway during summer, provide vibrant colour during autumn, and let the sun in during the winter months.

Dramatic Consequences

A composition of contrasting colours can also provide immediate drama to a garden. To achieve this effect, simply choose opposites from the colour wheel and place them beside each other for maximum contrast – blue hyacinths with orange marigolds, a hedge of red roses against their glossy green foliage, yellow tulips

A stunning row of golden elm *(Ulmus procera)* is underplanted with lush Agapanthus to guide visitors from the front gate to the house in this garden. The Agapanthus will provide greenery throughout the year with the added bonus of blue flowers during summer.

S. Kenny ; M. Stovar

This colourful corner, filled with *Ranunculus asiaticus*, pansies (*Viola x wittrockiana*), *Erigeron karvinskianus* and freesias (*Freesia hybrida*), is shown in both colour and black and white to demonstrate the part tone plays in how we see colours. Similar tones of different colours have been chosen in this planting, to give the garden a harmonious look, despite the different hues used.

with purple violets. Unfortunately, an entire garden based on this technique, though eye-catching, is anything but restful. Proportions are important. If equal amounts of both colours are used at full strength the result can be over the top – just the approach for those who seek a riot of colour in their gardens, but less impressive for those people looking for a charming atmosphere.

A more composed approach is to have a mass of a weaker colour contrasting with a small amount of a stronger colour. Try yellow daffodils with gold marigolds; red foliage with crimson roses; light blue hyacinths with deep blue hydrangeas.

However, it is important to remember that colours that seem to be very similar, such as two yellows, will look quite different if they are placed side by side, and colours that already look like opposites will look even more so when placed together.

Contrasting colours are used here to create a dramatic impact. The deep violet of the Dutch iris (*Iris x hollandica*) is made even more vivid by being planted next to bright yellow broom (*Genista* species).

Tonal Scale

While black and white are the extremes of tone, all colours can be reduced to a tonal scale. (To best appreciate this point, look at the black and white photo of a colourful garden bed above.)

Every colour has its own tonal depth. Yellow is lightest, followed by orange, then red and green, then blue and finally violet – the darkest tone. The red end of the spectrum has warm colours while the blue end has cool colours. A yellow colour theme can be cooled with a touch of blue or warmed with a little orange.

Grey can add tone to a garden bed, and create interesting effects when it is placed next to a strong colour. The grey actually takes on a tinge of the opposite colour on the colour wheel. For example, the grey becomes violet-tinged near yellow and if placed near red it turns greenish. However, if you're after a bright combination, choose the grey foliage

White valerian
(*Centranthus* 'Albus')
and mignonette,
(*Reseda odorata*) add
grace, elegance and
fragrance to this
country garden.

The pretty blue mealy sage (*Salvia farinacea*) is a moderately fast-growing perennial. A great bedding plant, it provides long-lasting colour in the garden and is also a lovely cut flower for indoors.

carefully as its addition can sometimes dull a planting. You should use silver-greys rather than lead-greys to keep colours strong.

A strong tone will always overwhelm adjacent gentler ones to the extent that the beauty of a subtly toned plant can be destroyed by vibrant neighbours. A mass planting of lavender can provide a delicate backdrop to a garden, only to be spoilt by a brightly coloured Rhododendron in the foreground.

For this reason, many gardeners find that white flower gardens free the designer from difficult colour decisions. If you feel confused by all the decisions involved in colour choices, stick to white. As well as being very fashionable, all-white gardens also enable us to concentrate on other plant qualities, such as perfume – a characteristic of many white flowers.

Structural Colour

However, we should not be afraid of colour and gardeners can learn to use it in small amounts until they feel more confident. In common garden structures such as fences and gates, bright hues can be especially appealing, showing that strident colour has a place. A wooden gate painted bright blue can uplift a tired old garden – as can a strongly coloured front fence.

Ugly colour clashes can occur – even in nature – so an understanding of colour theory is helpful. As a generalisation, blocks of bold, contrasting colours tend to suit formal approaches, while informality is more easily achieved with drifts of harmonious, pale colours. A hedge of brightly coloured plants such as azaleas is a favourite of many gardeners favouring the formal look, and provides a strong colour statement in spring. However, a cottage garden relies on informality and gardeners prefer to jostle different plants and colours in a relaxed fashion, relying on a paler colour palette to minimise clashing.

As for general colour tips, most gardeners like to use light-coloured flowers, such as yellow or white flowers to lighten up a dark garden. One particular favourite for dark shady areas is white busy lizzie (*Impatiens walleriana*), which grows easily in shady areas, self-seeds prolifically and is kept from becoming too leggy with simple pruning. It is also ideal for hanging baskets. Other possibilities include *Begonia semperflorens*, granny's bonnets (*Aquilegia vulgaris*) and white Agapanthus to add brightness to a shady spot.

White flowers are often useful for gardeners who favour brighter hues as they help provide a clear background. White flowers planted between blocks of coloured flowers defines the colours and keeps them separate. For example, pink flowers next to bright red tend to merge but if you place white flowers between them, the colours will remain distinct.

B. Wilson

The blue of this seat provides a delightful contrast to the masses of pastel love-in-a-mist and *Phlox paniculata* surrounding it.

Shades of Grey

Grey foliage can be both a practical and beautiful tool in good garden design. Many drought-hardy plants have grey leaves because their fine layer of hairs or waxy blooms protect them against drying out. Grey-foliaged plants can therefore be relied upon to perform in open, sunny situations. Indeed these plants mostly resent shade, especially when combined with moisture; in such conditions they suffer from fungal diseases such as sooty mould, a disease encouraged by the moisture trapped within the hairy leaf coverings. They prefer good air circulation and dislike being overcrowded.

Most of these plants will thrive even in difficult situations. In poor, stoney soils, well-drained or dry slopes, a wonderful garden of grey foliage is within the capacity of the most inexperienced of gardeners.

When used for visual effect, grey-foliaged plants also provide a softening effect on planting. They are especially useful in gardens with strong, unfiltered light as they offer relief from harsh, bright colours. Mediterranean-style gardens of silver-leaved olive trees, fragrant lavenders and clumped Artemisias need little more than your admiration to look good. And, if you have no desire to be a slave to your garden, they are the ideal choice.

A planting of silver-grey foliage in this charming courtyard garden, left, is used to great effect to soften the white-washed walls and green shutters. A weeping silver pear (*Pyrus salicifolia* 'Pendular') provides the focal point, surrounded by smaller plantings of white roses, lavender and delphiniums. Lamb's ear (*Stachys byzantina*) (1) has woolly grey foliage year-round and light mauve flowers in late spring. Silver feather (*Tanacetum ptarmiciflorum*) (2) has fern-like silvery foliage which is complemented by small daisy-like white flowers in summer. The silver tree (*Leucadendron argenteum*) (3), while not noted for its flowers, features grey leaves covered with short, white hairs – its foliage is popular in flower arrangements.

M. Stouar; D. Harvey

Designer Details

Inspiring gardeners

S. Kenny, garden of John and Georgina Ashworth, Cedar Brush Creek, NSW

Visiting the great gardens of the world has become a boom industry and it's easy to understand why when surrounded by their beauty. Whether you emulate their ideas, or merely admire the glory of the designs, a visit to the gardens designed by Gertrude Jekyll, Claude Monet, Edna Walling, Paul Sorensen or Vita Sackville-West, to name a few, will give you much to think about.

Open Garden Scheme

In 1987, the first year of the Australian Open Garden Scheme, 63 gardens in Victoria were included. Now the Open Garden Scheme embraces 700 gardens across the country.

The scheme offers the public the opportunity to see inspirational gardens at close range, and to share in the knowledge of the garden owners.

A brief description of the gardens, opening times and other relevant details are contained in the Open Gardens Scheme Guidebook which is available in late winter. Similar schemes also operate in New Zealand, England and Europe.

Gertrude Jekyll (1843-1932) ▲

The doyenne of the cottage garden movement was Gertrude Jekyll. Trained as an artist, she turned to gardening and writing because of failing eyesight and applied her colouring techniques to her beloved garden Munstead Wood in Surrey, England.

Gertrude Jekyll is broadly credited with the invention of the classic herbaceous perennial border. She preferred to plant long, thin drifts of one colour, reasoning that once a variety had ceased flowering the gap left in the border would be quickly filled by the plants in front and behind. Her borders were on a large scale and designed for large gardens.

She believed that grey foliage and white flowers alone were too bland and needed stengthening with a touch of blue or lemon-yellow. She also inspired many gardeners with her use of silver foliage as a foil for adjacent colours.

Together with eminent architect Sir Edwin Lutyens she advocated open air "rooms" and strong form in the gardens, providing vistas in all directions as structures for the garden.

"Eurambeen", Vic

J. Stouar

Edna Walling (1896-1973) ▲

Edna Walling was born in Yorkshire and trained in Melbourne, and was an admirer of the sophisticated designs of Gertrude Jekyll, particularly her soft colour schemes, but recognised that English gardens were inappropriate to Australian conditions.

Climate was of the utmost concern. Her love of Spanish and Italian gardens is evident in her surviving gardens with their vine-clad pergolas, shade trees, and paved outdoor living areas enclosed within low, stone walls. She integrated exotic species with native species in a casual style, and was one of the very first to promote an appreciation of Australian plants. She regularly extolled the virtues of green foliage, and surpassed all others in blending foliage, shape and texture. She emphasised structural framework and took her planting inspiration from nature.

Paul Sorensen (1890-1983) ▶

Paul Sorensen came to Australia in 1915 from Denmark as a qualified landscape architect with extensive European experience. Arriving during one of Australia's worst droughts he quickly recognised the value of water and always advised his clients: "Don't buy land, buy water." This was advice he followed, establishing a nursery in the Blue Mountains of New South Wales, on a site with a superb natural spring.

He grew a wide range of shrubs and trees which he used in his designs. Deciduous trees for autumn colour were favourites providing the backbone of a garden and he planted lavishly, while letting the site itself determine the layout. He liked to include existing views and Australian vegetation in his designs and used colour in broad sweeps, with subtle changes in foliage colour and texture to increase visual dimensions.

By good fortune, most of his commissions were for grand estates where he could indulge his planting passions.

S. Kenny

Aola, Peats Ridge, NSW

Sissinghurst ▶

When the husband and wife team of Harold Nicolson and Vita Sackville-West developed Sissinghurst in Kent, England, during the 1930s many of the ideas propounded by Gertrude Jekyll were explored. They wanted "the strictest formality of design with the maximum informality in planting" and they succeeded in creating one of the most visited gardens in England.

Superb high brick walls provided the formal framework, but perhaps the most famous section of Sissinghurst is the white garden, right, where silver- and grey-foliaged plants act as a buffer between white-flowering plants and dark green yew and box hedging. At its peak in the English summer it appears to shine and has become the role model for many gardens.

While some gardeners might argue that this safe approach, free from the concerns of bright colour combinations, has become hackneyed, the fact remains that for single-colour gardens white continues to be the firm favourite. Perhaps its popularity can be attributed to its luminescence and perfume at twilight.

Giverny ▶

Created by the great French Impressionist painter Claude Monet, over a period of 43 years, Giverny dazzles visitors with its displays. It is in fact two gardens – the water garden where Monet grew, and painted, his much-loved water lilies and the formal beds arranged as the foreground to the striking pink house.

Monet's beloved irises in varying shades of violet, purple, blue and white are massed to create swathes of colour, often more than 1m (3ft) wide in colour-themed beds. May is the perfect month to enjoy them; by June the colour has turned to mostly reds and rosy-pinks, achieved mainly with roses, especially climbers. There are also geraniums aplenty and many other species which achieve a dramatic visual display.

An extraordinary maintenance and planting program ensures there is abundant colour every day for the seven months it is open each year: 180,000 annuals are raised each year from seed and as many perennials planted. When the gates close in autumn, huge numbers of plants are dug up, potted and overwintered in glasshouses. Even the water lilies are dug annually from the drained pond, divided, and replaced in groups of three to achieve the desired summer display. A marvellous lesson in colour.

J. Stowar

Glorious Gardens

The rich reward of careful planning

◄ Hidcote

Major Lawrence Johnston developed the garden of Hidcote Manor in Gloucestershire, England, between 1907-1914. Considered to be the first garden masterpiece using the formula which was established by Gertrude Jekyll, it is today managed by the National Trust who also own the property.

Formal hedges provide the framework, creating vast areas and intimate spaces. Shaped plants abound and the garden is remarkable for these plants alone, without any colour other than green. However, the red border is perhaps the most interesting colour feature. Twin borders flank a pathway punctuated with small gazebos and a wrought-iron gate, inviting you to explore further.

A long, straight space does little to encourage the visitor to linger, however the theme of red flowers and purple-foliaged hazel in the foreground with backdrops of purple and coppery-foliaged plants such as Norway maple (Acer platanoides 'Crimson King',) is so refreshingly different, and successful, that it has become one of the garden's most admired features. This is a garden which manages to combine bright colour with good taste.

Natural Selection

Choosing plants to suit your garden

Good design depends on much more than just colour considerations. While praise has been given over the years to the cultivation of plants from regions quite alien to that of the gardener, things have changed. People now know that plants suited to the conditions of their area grow better. Many of these plants will be indigenous to the region and should perhaps form the garden's framework.

Birds, butterflies, frogs, lizards and smaller mammals are attracted by gardens that feature native habitats. As there is world-wide concern about the overuse of chemicals and the damage this can cause, the creation of garden habitats favoured by local bird species greatly reduces the need for pesticides.

However this approach does not necessarily exclude plants from other parts of the world which match your microclimate, soil, and drainage. It is simply a matter of careful planning and consideration.

Use Less Water

No matter where you are in the world, water for gardens is becoming more limited, so drought-hardiness should rank highly on your criteria when it comes to choosing plants. There are so many wonderful plants which can withstand extremely dry conditions for extended periods. Many plants from Mediterranean regions, such as lavender, are particularly suited to drier conditions.

Use these plants together with mulching and your garden will not become a burden. A garden should require no more of your time than you are happy to give.

Grevillea 'Superb'

S. Kenny, Paradise Plants, Kulnura NSW; A. Stewart

Camellias, such as these *Camellia sasanqua* 'Kangiro', right, are a favourite with many gardeners because of their low maintenance. They don't need pesticides and they thrive in dry conditions. The Australian-bred lavender, 'Sidonie' makes a attractive display beneath the Camellias.

An eye-catching display of conifers, left, includes white cedar (*Thuja occidentalis*), Spanish fir (*Abies pinsapo* 'Aurea'), false cypress (*Chamaecyparis nootkatensis compacta*) and three different junipers. Several tiers have been created, above right, with the use of straight-edged conifers, rounded, shrubby roses, foxgloves, various trees, a hedging of Buxus, and a flourish of *Erigeron karvinskianus*.

S. Kenny, Quindalup, Boaral, NSW; R. Hyett (above)

Good Form

Plant shape and form are the features that you will look at year-round and so should receive close attention when planning your garden. Beautiful flower colour is a bonus to be enjoyed only after the overall plant shapes and groupings are established.

Plants are rarely seen in isolation, so associations become very important. Plant groupings often become memorable through repetition of species. Try not to use plants singularly. Many designers find an odd number of plants to be the best – three tall conifers in a row, five colourful hibiscus in a section of the garden.

However, you need to think about how much repetition is desirable before the scheme becomes boring. Variety can be important, but when a garden has too much contrast or variety, chaos will reign.

When planning a garden, sketch out a rough plan on graph paper – look at the garden as a whole, not just in small pieces. One of the most common mistakes people make is to visit a large nursery, buy whatever takes their fancy and come home with a mixture of plants, pots and flowers and no idea of where or how to plant them.

Look at your garden's existing plants and use them as a starting point. Do they provide a good basic structure? Think about how they will look in a couple more years and whether they should be gradually replaced. Don't rip everything out at once unless it is really awful. Try to work on things gradually, so you can slowly move to the desired design without leaving gaping holes in your surroundings in the meantime.

Room to Move

Imagine having to remove a well-established plant from the garden after years of nurturing, because it has outstripped its allotted space. Sometimes this is because its performance has far exceeded that anticipated, but usually it's because not enough attention was given to the initial choice.

The mature size of plants (both height and spread) is often underestimated and many garden books and some plant labels are negligent in this respect. Part of the dilemma rests with the actual growing conditions. Ask advice from as many people as possible before making decisions about your main trees and shrubs. Look for mature specimens in your local parks and gardens to give you further guidance.

It is wrong to plant a jacaranda or deodar cedar only 1m (3ft) from a driveway, or a weeping fig with rampageous roots above a sewer line, knowing that you will have moved on in 5 or 10 years time. Trees should be for posterity.

Take a good look at the area you plan to plant. Note where the shadows fall during the day and at different times of the year. Don't automatically sacrifice sunlight to provide some privacy in your garden. Deciduous trees can be a good compromise by providing shade in summer and allowing light in winter, while evergreens are perfect for year-round privacy.

Ground space requirements should be carefully considered with shrubs, too. Why constantly prune shrubs when you can select others more suited to the space that need only an occasional trimming? It doesn't always mean compromising on your favourite plant choices. Many popular plants, such as Camellias, azaleas, lavender and roses, have dwarf species which will provide the colour you want in a smaller space.

Compact varieties of *Camellia sasanqua* such as 'Paradise Petite' perform well as an informal screen which follows the line of a garden path, right, or can be clipped into a more formal hedge to add structure to the garden, above.

J. Stouar

Jacarandas, left, are one of the most spectacular flowering trees for warmer climates. But beware, they need plenty of room to move. Rhododendrons, below, can provide a range of great colours in the garden but do develop into spreading shrubs. Give them plenty of room to grow, unless you are prepared to prune regularly. Low-growing plants such as sage and Erigeron are perfect for lining paths, right, as unlike shrubs, they are not likely to take over and interfere with the space required on the path. They will also provide a nice contrasting outline for the paving stones.

Hyett

Perfect Paths

One of the most common garden layout mistakes is that of inadequate path widths. The minimum you should aim for is 2m (6ft), as this allows for plants to spill out on either side and still leave room for people to pass. In established gardens where shrubs have far exceeded the available ground space, a solution is to "lift" the canopy by removing lower foliage and revealing the stems.

When planning a garden, it is important to note where people are most likely to walk and plan the paths accordingly. It is often best just to use the most direct route to and from the front and back doors rather than planning complex pathways.

If you do want to put in a winding path, it is best to use paving, bricks, stone or another medium to highlight the outline of the path and ensure visitors keep to the intended route. Otherwise you may find that after some time, people will cut corners and end up walking over the garden beds, destroying all your careful planning and nurturing.

This mass of golden Cosmos provides a brilliant display and will readily self-seed, ensuring bright colour for years.

Quick Fixes

Instant colour with annuals and perennials

Faced with a barren block around a newly-built house, it's a common reaction to fill it with colour using mass-planted annuals. Within weeks the area can be transformed. But it is a short-lived display and unfortunately an expensive one when you purchase annuals by the punnet. Germinating your own seedlings from purchased seed is far cheaper but more demanding of time and effort.

By cutting back your annuals immediately after flowering, then fertilising, you may get a second flush of flowers. However, much depends on timing and weather conditions. Good value annuals are those which readily self-sow – marigolds, Californian poppies, Cosmos, nasturtiums, Impatiens, heartsease, love-in-the-mist and hollyhocks – which will sometimes surprise you where they reappear. And while colour combinations will be spontaneous and unstructured, they will be no less appealing for it.

Budget-conscious gardeners are now turning to soft-wood perennials – plants which, once established, develop into clumps which can be divided and spread throughout the garden. These include Agapanthus, Aquilegia, Physostegia, Diascia, Gazania and Arctotis. If suited to your site conditions, you will have

Snapdragon (*Antirrhinum majus*)

Obedient plant (*Physostegia virginiana* 'Vivid'), above left, has mauve flowers and makes a good autumn cut flower. Other colourful favourites include *Eschscholzia californica* and African daisies (*Dimorphotheca*), centre, and the fragrant and colourful heartsease, (*Viola tricolor*), right.

progeny from those first purchases forever more! So while initial costs may be higher than for annuals, in the longer term they are very economical. Soft-wood perennials (named because they don't contain woody tissue and so can't grow very tall), are suited to every garden situation.

Rapid Multiplication

Always prepare the soil thoroughly for soft-wood perennials with organic matter and fertiliser. Their multiplication will then be rapid and for most, the display will be colourful in the first season. With other species, flowering will occur from the second year onwards.

Regular deadheading and cutting back after flowering, combined with fertilising, will encourage repeat flowerings. Most species will need lifting and dividing every few years, so you will always have spare plants to pass to friends. A garden bed of these perennials can be designed for maximum colour impact at one season or you can mix plants for interest at all times of the year. In those cases, "foliage" plants will be relied on to hold the scheme together. A favourite is Buxus which can be clipped into topiary or used as a hedge to give a garden strong form and design.

S. Kenny, Gledswood Homestead, NSW

Borrowed Landscapes

*H*ighlighting a view or a distant feature of the garden can be achieved by the selective use of colour. If you want to make the most of the "borrowed" landscape - that is what stretches beyond the boundaries of your garden, it may be a distant vista or nearby tree in an adjoining yard - avoid placing any bright or warm colour in the foreground because it will divert your attention.

If your garden has a view of the ocean or a bushland backdrop, choose foliage or flowering plants that complement these environments, white, green, grey or pale blues will work best. Consider the cushion bush (Caloccphalus brownii) or coastal rosemary (Westringia fruticosa) and plant them in a border to frame or draw attention to the outlook.

Blues and greens are well-suited to backgrounds as they visually retreat; they will enlarge the appearance of a garden and highlight a distant view whereas flowers and plants from the warm colour range will create a focus, making this aspect of the garden appear much closer to you.

This garden features low-growing perennials so as not to detract from the expansive views, left. Pyrethrum daisies (*Tanacetum coccineum*) make a colourful and fragrant border as does catmint (*Nepeta x faassenii*) and a low hedge of lavender in the background.
The vibrant colours of Ageratum and Cosmos, far left, shine against white Agapanthus.

Light Fantastic

The effects of light on colour

To the English visitor, the clear, bright Australian light is startling, particularly in summer when the harsh contrasts and violent shadows are the order of the day. The Australian artist Sidney Nolan said the key to Australian landscapes was the light, because it had an incandescence which gave the sky more significance than the landscape itself.

There is a crispness of definition but harsh light from some surfaces results in glare and strong hues can easily become bleached out. The more intense the light, the greater the need for intense colour.

Colour Intensity

For this reason, the colours of traditional garden flowers often appear washed out in Australia. Pastel colours in Australia's midday sun look feeble, whereas in the soft, bluish light of England they glow. Red and yellow flowers seem to gain in colour intensity in the strong Australian light, and white flowers become highly reflective. The brightness of white flowers in the midday sun can be softened by the introduction of silver or grey foliage and red or yellow flowers can be interspersed with green foliage so they don't appear too warm.

To enliven an English winter, gardeners rely heavily on silver, gold and variegated foliage but in Australia the bright effects of light on gold foliage is almost too much. So while golden foliage can be very useful in brightening a garden corner, discretion is needed with its use so it does not overpower the garden. The native grey-greens of Australia are far easier to live with in this harsher light, so it's fortunate that these tones tend to dominate our natural environment.

A beautiful show of *Dimorphotheca* hybrids becomes more intense in colour when positioned under a shady tree.

Leafy Surroundings

Foliage as a garden feature

Never underestimate the importance of foliage in your garden design. Excluding plant shape, it is the characteristic that's on show for most of the year, and has far more significance than flowers, as it offers colour and texture.

Texture, the surface quality, is dependent on leaf size. Large-leaved plants such as Acanthus, some Philodendrons, Monsteras and Cannas have coarse textures, while small-leaved plants such as tea-trees, thymes and most grasses have fine textures. Bold-foliaged plants appear to advance towards us. Therefore, in a plant grouping, it is wise to place large-leaved plants in front and use those with finer textures at the back to maintain a sense of depth.

Using foliage in this way can be a very effective means of creating a sense of depth in small gardens when the space may be quite limited. For dramatic effect nothing beats a single bold-foliaged plant in a small space, particularly a walled courtyard. The remarkable monks' purgative (*Gunnera manicata*), when given the moisture it needs, is without parallel. Dramatic contrast can be achieved by grouping just one large-leaved plant with a collection of small-leaved plants. The reverse also applies.

In the wild, leaf size is closely related to habitat. Tropical plants are characterised by large, shiny leaves – the large leaf surface being necessary to fulfill the plant's photosynthetic needs, often under poor light conditions beneath the rainforest canopy.

In open, sunny situations, especially in arid areas, fine-foliaged plants predominate, the small leaf size reflecting the need to reduce leaf surface and therefore moisture loss.

In gardens where we carelessly mix fine

Canna x generalis

The red tones of a Japanese maple (*Acer palmatum*) and the dramatic dark purple Cotinus foliage provide a contrasting background for the the blue juniper (*Juniperus x media*). Note the clever use of the finer-textured foliages to provide textural harmony in this grouping.

S. Kenny, Buskers End, Bowral, NSW

and bold foliages, the results can be aesthetically disturbing. For example, conifers are fine-textured and can look incongruous in a garden of lush-leaved tropicals. Try to select plants from similar environmental conditions for at least each section of your garden.

Make the most of the endless variations of green foliages. Create depth and interest in your garden using shades of green. Place the lighter ones to the foreground and the deepest to the background with the mid-shades in-between. This graduation in tone will result in greater visual depth.

Coloured Foliage

Deep green foliage is always the safest garden backdrop because a piece of sculpture or any flowering plant will have most impact against this backdrop. Pale greens such as in plants like *Pittosporum* 'Irene Patterson' and *Pittosporum* 'James Stirling' demand our attention when the surroundings are deep greens.

Purple-bronze foliages recede even further and in small gardens should be placed to the rear of a grouping to accentuate depth. Most purple-bronze plants turn greenish in shady situations

The bold palm-like Fatsia leaves contrast with maidenhair fern (*Adiantum* species) and Pteris ferns with a dark green *Bergenia cordifolia* in the foreground.

and will still provide some colour. For sheer visual pleasure the combination of purple foliage with pink foliage or flowers is very satisfying. Purple foliage often works well with green, too.

To illuminate an already overshadowed garden corner, use light-coloured foliages. Grey, silver and gold foliage is a very effective contrast when used in this way. One of the most serviceable grey-foliaged plants for frost-free situations is *Helichrysum petiolare*, a very fast-growing shrub with a characteristic horizontal spread. The form 'Limeglow' is, as the name implies, brighter, but is also more shade-tolerant than the commonly seen grey variety.

In cool climate gardens maples are useful plants for shaded areas, performing well despite the low levels of light beneath canopies. Those with lime-green leaves such as *Acer japonicum* 'Aureum' are doubly effective.

In bright light, gold foliage should be used with a great deal of restraint. It can easily be overdone in Australian gardens, resulting in them looking even hotter under sun-drenched summer skies. One gold-foliaged plant can be eye-catching when surrounded by green ones but this impact is lost with the repetitive use of gold foliage.

Purple and gold foliage placed side by side, while initially dramatic, becomes disturbing if used to excess as the contrast is too great. The resulting garden is anything but restful. Unfortunately, one of the most commonly seen plant associations is golden diosma (*Coleonema pulchrum* 'Sunset Gold') with red-foliaged sacred bamboo (*Nandina domestica*). This is garden exhibitionism at its worst, not only because of the vivid colour contrast but also because both colours seem to advance towards the viewer.

Successful Partnerships

♦ *Cotinus coggyria* '**Purpurea**' *(Purple smoke bush) and* **Euphorbia wulfenii**
♦ *Corylus maxima* '**Purpurea**' *(Purple hazel) and* **Ajuga reptans** '**Jungle Beauty**'
♦ *Echium fastuosum* *(Beebalm) and* **Euphorbia wulfenii**
♦ *Cotinus coggyria* '**Purpurea**' *and* **Raphiolepis x delacourii** *(Pink Indian hawthorn)*
♦ *Helichrysum petiolare* '**Limeglow**' *and* **Salvia ambigens** *(Sage)*

Golden oregano (*Origanum*), above, adds interesting texture and colour to a garden and is wonderfully aromatic; it can be used in cooking, too. Japanese maples (*Acer palmatum*), above right, provide a variety of leaf shapes and colours. Care needs to be taken when using plants such as golden diosma (*Coleonema pulchrum* 'Sunset Gold'), below, so it does not become overpowering.

Continuous Colour

Conifers for year-round interest

Conifers are one of the most primitive groups of plants, having evolved over hundreds of millions of years. Their hardiness perhaps derives from this long and illustrious history.

Many of the well known conifers in cultivation have arisen from cool climate species in the northern hemisphere. The varieties featured on this page fit into this cool climate category, so don't expect them to perform as well in warm, temperate or subtropical climates.

For warmer climates there are alternatives such as plum pines (*Podocarpus* species) for smaller gardens or Araucarias such as bunya pine or Norfolk Island pine for larger gardens.

The needle-like foliage reduces water loss so all conifers are quite hardy and able to withstand dry periods. They are an excellent choice for large gardens as they act as a background plant providing solid colour in a range of greens, yellows and blues to frame flowering plants in the foreground. The results can be spectacular.

S Kenny Bushers End and Oxindabun Bowral NSW

Blue spruce (*Picea pungens*)

Pfitzer juniper (*Juniperus x media*)

Blue atlas cedar (*Cedrus atlantica* 'Glauca')

Blue spruce (*Picea pungens*)

A collection of conifers

R. Hyett

***Photinia glabra* 'Rubens'**

Leaves Which Change Colour as They Age

*T*here are a number of fabulous species which produce intense red, pink or orange tones in their new foliage. It is thought that the anthocyanin pigments which create these bright colours evolved to convince animals that this succulent tender new growth should be left alone and not devoured by them.

Of course we humans do not normally graze on this new growth but it does have exceptional value as an attractive spring feature, particularly when it comes to hedge or topiary plants. Photinia glabra 'Rubens' is perhaps the best of all when it comes to bright red new leaves. It is perfect for hedges as it grows to about 3m (9ft) by about 2m (6ft) wide and responds brilliantly to pruning. It is moderately frost-tolerant and adaptable to a wide variety of soil types. Its white flowers are also attractive, if unspectacular, in spring.

The Australian lilly pillies are another outstanding example of a group of plants providing colourful foliage. Known botanically as Syzygium and Acmena there are dozens of species of lilly pilly including a number which originate in the tropical parts of south-east Asia. The species from the more temperate regions of southern Australia provide some of the most useful topiary and hedge plants. A few reliable favourites are the scrub cherry (Syzygium australe), the brush cherry (S. paniculatum) and the creek lilly pilly (Acmena smithii). These plants will grow into small trees if left to their own devices but of course their great quality is that they can be heavily pruned into whatever shape you desire.

Another great feature of the lilly pillies is the colourful fruits they produce in summer. These fruits come in a variety of colours from white to purple to red and the pulp is edible. The bronze to red-coloured new growth of all species is perhaps their outstanding feature in springtime; new flushes of this colour can be encouraged through regular pruning in spring and summer. Their use for topiary and their adaptability has made them a most popular plant, however they do need protection from heavy frosts.

The mottled bark of the Crepe myrtle (*Lagerstroemia indica*) provides a striking winter feature.

Trusses of pastel pink, lilac or white flowers adorn the branches of the crepe myrtle tree in summer.

Spring-flowering pink *Erica* shines against the variegated *Rhododendron* 'President Roosevelt'.

Seasonal Shades

Colour throughout the year

We are often lured into buying plants when they are in flower, and while there is no shame in giving in to this impulse, spare a thought for your existing garden before you succumb.

Consider whether the plant has colour features at other times of the year, such as autumn leaf tones or brightly coloured berries. The crepe myrtle group, for example, provides year-round interest. These small trees boast a variety of pastel-coloured flowers which are borne in late summer and autumn. In late autumn the leaves of some turn fiery red, orange or yellow while in winter the leafless trees provide delightful patterns of colour with their patchy bark. Alternatively, the Pigeon berry (*Duranta repens*) bears sky-blue flowers in summer and yellowish-orange berries in autumn and winter.

Added Interest

The challenge is to imagine your garden at every stage of the year and not focus solely on the spring blooms or other times when there is much colour. Plan for a succession of interesting effects. Camellias in winter, annuals in spring, perennials in summer and deciduous trees and shrubs in autumn are just a few examples of how you can create a picture in your garden that will last all year. The plant world is so incredibly diverse that you can explore colour for a lifetime and still only sample a fraction of the possibilities! However, before you decide on a plant or a position, consult the table at the back of this book for ideas and inspiration.

Ceratostigma willmottianum, above and left, performs all year round. Closely related to Plumbago, its brilliant blue flowers in summer give way to fruits and fiery red leaves in late autumn.

Don't be restricted to using traditional pots to add colour to outdoor areas. These pretty antique urns are filled with Million Bells 'Blue Chimes' petunia hybrids, which produce masses of small vibrant flowers throughout spring, summer and autumn.

Pots of Colour

Brightening up corners and courtyards

Pots and containers of all descriptions have become extremely popular as gardens have shrunk in size over the last few decades. With the trend towards urban consolidation, people are living in smaller homes and courtyards and balconies have become the gardens of the nineties.

Growing plants in containers provides wonderful opportunities for the colour conscious, as not only do we design with plants but also the containers themselves can be quite a fashion accessory. It is possible now to get pots in all shapes, sizes and colours and it is worth considering this aspect before commencing a container garden. If a large number of containers are to be used then some co-ordination of colours and textures will give a much more pleasant effect. Consider the surface that the containers will be placed upon, whether that be paving, terracotta bricks, or a wooden verandah, and try to match the container with it for best effect. The many different options are covered thoroughly in The Australian Women's Weekly Garden Guide *The Potted Garden*.

The nursery industry has changed dramatically in recent times, and there is now an overwhelming emphasis on "potted colour", even to the extent of co-ordinating the colour of

Federation daisies

the pot and the flower in it to appeal to our sense of instant aesthetics. Some of this "instant colour" is provided by very quick growing annuals such as pansies, petunias and snapdragons in pots and such material is very much a disposable product, lasting only a few weeks or months.

While these plants obviously have a place, in order to avoid disappointment, the consumer should be well aware that they are buying a short-term solution. There are many other plants which are suitable for long-term cultivation in pots and if the right plants are chosen you can look forward to years of pleasure. Decide what your aims are in designing with colourful plants. Disposable pot plants of the sort mentioned above can be used in much the same way as a bunch of flowers; you can choose whatever colourful arrangement takes your fancy and if it doesn't look quite right on the table or mantlepiece, then no great damage has been done. Long-term pots, however, deserve much more detailed consideration as they often involve a considerable investment of time and money.

The Right Container

Perhaps the most important decision to make when you are looking at container growing is how long-term the planting will be. Do you

S. Kenny: urns from The Country Trader, Paddington; terracotta pots from Parkers of Turramurra, NSW

S. Kenny; pots from Parkers of Turramurra, NSW

A row of potted *Cuphea llavea* 'Tiny Mice', above, provides a brilliant welcome at an entrance. A planting of white tulips and primulas in a white pot, left, lightens a shaded backyard.

A. Martin

want the container to last for many years, or is it to be just a temporary planting to be disposed of when it starts to look shabby? An alternative is to pot a long-term plant and underplant it with an annual or bulb which can be changed at the end of its growing season.

The best plants to consider for long-term pot culture are those that renew their root system each year, such as bulbs and herbaceous perennials (perennial plants which die back to ground level each year and then subsequently produce a new root and shoot system the following growing season). Examples of such plants include daffodils, irises, asters, Agapanthus, Aquilegias, Anemones, Delphiniums, diascias as well as many others. The range of colours is virtually limitless so let the artist in you run wild on your potted canvas. These plants will continue to expand in a pot but the beauty of them is that you will be able to split the plants up and repot them and they should come back better than ever. Quite shallow pots can be used for these plants given that the plants do not have an extensive root system.

Shrubs in Pots

Shrubs, on the other hand, such as Gardenias and Camellias, are suitable for the medium term, but the problem is that their root system continues to expand each year as the plant increases in height. Eventually the root system runs out of space and starts to die. Of course you can repot the plants into larger and larger pots each year but this is not a permanent solution.

Trees are in the same category but the problem is even worse as they tend to grow to larger heights in quicker time. Nonetheless, if you accept that trees and shrubs may have a limited pot life before they need to be replaced, then you can still use them to great advantage in your potted garden; decorate an area for a time and then plant them in the garden before they become root bound. However, if you really can't do without

A. Martin

A pot of tulips provides a flourish of spring colour in this cool climate garden. Tulip bulbs look terrific in containers but they need pre-chilling for best flowering results. Bulbs are great for pots because they don't have extensive root systems.

Some roses, such as 'Carabella', provide glorious potted colour.

A large container of pale pink Rhodendron set against trailing Wisteria blossoms creates a beautiful canvas of spring colour.

that Gardenia or Camellia choose a dwarf or ground covering type such as *Gardenia augusta* 'Radicans' or *Camellia sasanqua* 'Little Liane' which have smaller root systems.

Moveable Colour

Plants such as bulbs and annuals lend themselves well to providing colour which can be easily moved into the house. Because of their small size and limited root systems they grow to perfection in small pots. The key to success is understanding their growing cycles.

Bulbs are planted at the beginning of their growing season. For most spring-flowering bulbs such as daffodils, tulips, freesias, and hyacinths, this means planting in autumn. For most summer and autumn-flowering bulbs such as gladioli, belladonna lilies or golden spider lilies, planting will be in spring or early summer. Once bulbs start to grow they should be regularly fed and watered.

Annuals need to be planted at the start of their growing season and be kept well-fed and watered. Most bulbs and annuals need an outdoor position in full sun to bring them to flowering stage, after which they can be brought indoors. Bury pots to the top of the pot rim in a garden bed to lessen the watering that needs to be done by hand. When the plant reaches full flower, the pot can be dug up, washed off and moved to its place.

A. Martin

A mass planting of grape hyacinth (*Muscari armeniacum*), above, enlivens an old wheelbarrow in early spring.

Curious Containers

A good way to create a colourful feature in the garden is to use an imaginative container such as an old wheelbarrow, laundry tub, wooden wine barrel, hollow log, or tea pot. An unusual container will draw the eye and accentuate whatever is planted in it, so choose wisely when selecting the plants. They should not only blend with the container but also with any plants that might sit behind the planting in the garden. Resist the temptation to plant a mass of bright colour; it might clash with your existing garden. Make sure there are plenty of drainage holes in the container (a hole every 10cm [4in] or so). If it's a long-term planting, it is a good idea to mix 20 percent weed-free top soil into your potting mix. This is important because most commercial potting mixes are based on organic matter and over time they tend to compact and lose a lot of their air spaces. Some good crumbly top soil will help the mix in the long term. It is also a good idea to sprinkle some slow release fertiliser over the surface of the mix every few months as most commercial potting mixes will only have enough fertiliser in them to last a few months.

The subtle tones of Russian sage (*Perovskia atriplicifolia* 'Longin'), contrast beautifully with the warm terracotta-washed walls of this house.

A planting of pansies (*Viola x wittrockiana*), *Lobelia trigonocaulis* and alyssum (*Lobularia maritima*).

Window Boxes

Garden space is at a premium in densely populated cities in many areas of Europe so window boxes are a particularly popular decoration. They give us a chance to complement the colour scheme of the building with a splash of natural colour and texture, and allow us the opportunity to experiment with the colour of the window box by painting it; but think carefully about the colour scheme of your wall and that of the plants you are going to grow before you take up a brush.

There are a few basic points to follow to ensure success with window boxes. First consider the aspect of the window box and how much sunlight it will receive, remembering that the position of the sun varies substantially during the course of the year. In summer the sun is much higher in the sky, resulting in more sunlight, while the opposite is

Kalanchoe

true in winter. This will make it easier to choose the best type of plant for growing in any particular situation. As window boxes are often attached to a wall, they can be influenced by microclimatic effects such as being a little protected from frosts, winds and rain.

Window boxes have a tendency to dry out quicker than plants in the open garden so it is very important to use a high quality potting mix specifically designed for outdoor pot plants. It is also a very good idea to check whether your potting mix has added fertiliser or not. If not, then you should either feed the plants every two weeks with a soluble complete fertiliser or add some slow release fertiliser, following the manufacturer's recommendation. In addition it is well worth adding moisture-saving crystals or a similar product to the mix to further reduce the water stress on the plants growing in the window box.

Paradise New Guinea Impatiens

Pick *of the* Bunch

The best plants for container colour

Agapanthus *If you are looking for a tough-as-nails plant for a sun-baked window box then the dwarf varieties of Agapanthus such as Agapanthus 'Blue Baby' are an excellent selection. There is a choice between either soft purple or snow white and the flower stems reach a height of approximately 60cm (2ft). The plants cope very readily with the neglect that busy working people sometimes inadvertently inflict on them. They flower in mid-summer and the waxy bell-shaped flowers last for several weeks.*

Brachycomes *These dainty little Australian daisies are extremely rewarding as potted plants due to their ability to flower for most of the year. Brachycome multifida and its cultivars such as 'Pink Haze', 'Blue Haze' and 'Break o' day' provide compact little mounds of deep green feathery foliage with masses of tiny daisy flowers in purple, mauve, pink*

Viola x wittrockiana

or white for the designer looking for pastel colours. Plants are easily renewed by taking tip cuttings at any time of the year.

Clivias *One of God's great gifts to gardeners is the kaffir lily (Clivia miniata). This hardy low-maintenance plant has the ability to illuminate densely shaded areas with its warm orange flowers. It produces its clumps of deep green strap-like leaves in the same fashion as the ever-popular Agapanthus and*

it will even thrive when planted in those difficult shaded positions beneath evergreen trees. It flowers in spring and the only maintenance necessary is to cut off the spent flower stems, although you may want to wait until the spectacular red seed pods have fallen.

Daffodils and jonquils *For a burst of late winter and spring colour you can't go past these beautiful and often fragrant bulbs. They can be massed effectively in a single planting or by combining a number of varieties. The Narcissus genus is divided into 12 divisions and the flowers range from the sweetly scented jonquil (Narcissus 'Cheerfulness') to the large trumpet daffodil (Narcissus 'Spellbinder'). Pots of daffodils and jonquils can be brought into the house while they are in flower and the pretty bulbs also create a beautiful window box display.*

A. Martin; S. Kenny; A. Stewart

Dahlias Various dwarf-growing Dahlias are available for pot culture and they will provide a lovely array of bright, bold oranges, yellows and reds. These are raised from seed and should be planted in spring for summer/autumn flowering.

Dianthus There are many worthy dwarf varieties of Dianthus Brachycome 'Sunburst' suitable for pots. The garden pinks (Dianthus plumarius) grow to about 30cm (1ft) with a similar spread. They are frost hardy perennials that flower in late spring and are lovely as cut flowers.

Gazanias For those difficult areas near the coast, the treasure flower (Gazania x hybrida) is an excellent choice. The large daisy flowers are produced in a range of bright bold colours from yellow to white to orange and often the centres have black markings which contrast beautifully with the petals. They are hardy clump-forming perennials or annuals which have shiny green leaf tops and silvery contrasting under-surfacing. They are also drought-resistant and make a great choice if there is a likelihood that watering will not be frequent.

Hyacinths These highly fragrant gems provide one of the most popular plants for indoor pot displays with their soft range of pastel colours. Bulbs are readily purchased in autumn and can be grown in shallow containers for spring displays. The bulbs can even be suspended above a container of water and the roots will grow down

Petunia x hybrida

into it providing a real novelty for the house. One word of caution with hyacinths – the skin (or tunic) of the bulb can cause skin irritation in some people so it is best to wear gloves when planting.

Impatiens For plants that will flower in lots of shade it is hard to ignore the various types of Impatiens. They are all very easy to strike from tip cuttings and the colours range from white to pink to purple and red. They are frost-tender, so in harsh climates it is wise to go for the annual types such as Impatiens walleriana which can be grown from seed to flower in a matter of a few weeks. In warm climates the perennial New Guinea hybrids can be grown. These have much larger flowers in a wider range of colours, even bicolours such as pale and dark pink.

Pansies Once again, an incredible variety of colours is available in everything from soft blues to yellows, reds, oranges and

even black for a really strong contrast with other colours in the garden. Pansies can flower from winter right through to late summer by having a succession of plantings every three months or so.

Petunias These fast growing annuals are one of the most rewarding plants for container culture. Like Agapanthus they seemingly thrive on neglect although a little care will provide handsome rewards. Separate colour strains are available in everything from pink, white, mauve, purple, red, even yellow. If planted early in spring they will flower right through summer and autumn, just trim them back after each flush of flowers, fertilise, and they will be off again.

Salvia For those who cannot resist a bold statement in red then the bonfire salvia (Salvia splendens) is high on the list. Dwarf strains which grow to only 30cm (1ft) are available and their bold upright spires of fire engine red are produced through summer and autumn. They should be planted in spring and will benefit greatly from regular pinching of the growing tips when they are young.

Sweet alyssum (Lobularia maritima) This hardy annual is fast growing and has masses of small pom-pom-shaped flower heads in white, pink or mauve. Seeds should be planted in spring for colour right through summer and autumn. The plants should be deadheaded to promote continuous flowering.

Brachycome 'Sunburst'

Impatiens walleriana

1

2

3

High Society

Climbing colour in the garden

Some of the most spectacular flowering plants are climbers which sprawl over trees in their natural habitats to reach full sunlight. They are incredibly useful for providing colour in small gardens as they usually do not provide the sort of root problems that trees do. However, there are some exceptions to this rule such as Wisteria which has very invasive roots and can cause damage to foundations and sewer lines. A virtually limitless range of colours, forms and textures can be found within the climbers. It is matter of establishing what sort of colour you want in your garden and which season that colour will feature.

Bright, gaudy colours from lolly pinks to reds, yellows and oranges can be provided in warm climates by the Bougainvilleas. The Jacaranda family (*Bignoniacceae*) provides numerous colourful warm climate creepers such as the orange trumpet vine (*Pyrostegia venusta*), the bower of beauty (*Pandorea jasminoides*) with its subtle trumpets, or the riotous pink sprays of the Port St John creeper (*Podranea ricasoliana*). For cooler climates the pastel shades of the many forms of Clematis are well worth considering. A visit to your local nursery is probably the best way to find the right climber for your garden.

Climbers are generally easy to grow but it is worth remembering that most need full sun to flower at their best. Also make sure to provide appropriate support such as a trellis or fence. Allowing the plants to climb on trees and shrubs might look stunning but all too often it means that you are condemning the support plant to a slow, painful and lingering death.

Trailing colour is always a great way to enliven verandah posts, gateways, garden sheds and pergolas. This bright Clematis (1) provides striking summer colour to an otherwise quiet garden area. An ornamental grape vine such as this glory vine (2) is another easy-to-grow alternative. Added interest is provided by the fruit in summer. Wisteria (3) is a perennial favourite, with its cascading fragrant blooms but be careful not to plant where it will use important structures for support, or it may bring everything, including the house, down! The pretty banksia rose (*Rosa banksiae lutea*) (4) offers clusters of fluffy butter-yellow flowers and its vigor, hardiness and lack of thorns makes it a popular choice for gardeners. It takes no time to transform an arch into a blooming canopy.

R. Hyett

B. Wilson

A potted cumquat (*Fortunella*) is a stunning feature next to this sandstone archway.

Fruits of Labour

Introducing colour with fruit and berries

Many plants offer colourful fruits as an added bonus at the end of a flowering season. The function of these colourful fruits is, of course, to attract animals who eat the fruits and disperse the seeds to other locations. It is no coincidence then that many of the most colourful fruits are in the red, orange and yellow groups, as these are particularly attractive to birds.

Care is needed when selecting colourful fruiting plants for the garden, as some of them can become wild when the seed is widely distributed. Cotoneasters, well-known for their bright displays of reds and oranges in autumn, have become an environmental weed in parts of Australia. Lantana was originally introduced as a hedge plant for gardens but the attractive black berries

Schefflera actinophylla

have ensured that its seed is widely distributed and it is now a problem weed in many parts of the world.

Having said that, there are only a small number of species which cause problems but it is worth checking whether any such problems exist in your area.

One of the best features of colourful fruits is that they are generally produced in autumn or winter when there is not much in the way of flowers in the garden. It is important to consider what other colours will be around when the plants are in fruit, so that a harmonious blend can be established. The dramatic reds of some berries can be used to create interesting contrasts, with the strong orange and yellow foliage of deciduous trees or with the white trunk of a silver birch, which will be losing its leaves when the berries are at their best.

S. Kenny; A. Stewart

Cordyline stricta

Cordyline rubra

Berberis 'Rubrostilla'

Cordyline cannifolis

Berried Treasure

Attract birds and achieve a burst of autumn and winter colour by adding these plants to your garden.

Citrus *Many gardeners consider Citrus as purely functional plants rather than highly ornamental trees and shrubs. Most Citrus have perfumed pinky-white flowers, glossy dark green leaves and brightly coloured fruit. The cumquat Fortunella margarita, with its small orange fruits, is perhaps the best for small gardens and containers. If space is at a premium, the Tahitian lime (Citrus aurantifolia) is a compact tree with greenish-yellow fruits. None of the Citrus group grows to more than 15m (45ft).*

Crataegus (Hawthorn) *There are literally hundreds of different types of hawthorns, most of which are deciduous and bear prominent thorns. Another feature is their colourful fruits: mainly in shades of red or yellow and either held singly or in clusters. Crataegus x smithiana has bright scarlet berries for about four months from late autumn to winter.*

Duranta erecta (Pigeon berry) *This plant is popular in warmer climates with its sky-blue flowers in summer and orange-yellow autumn berries. A dense evergreen shrub, it makes a great screen plant.*

Elaeocarpus reticulatus (Blueberry ash) *This wonderful small tree bears a mass of almost iridescent blue berries which are preceded by cup-shaped small flowers with intricately fringed petals. The flowers also have an aniseed perfume.*

Nandina domestica (Sacred bamboo) *This clump-forming plant provides a bamboo-like effect without the rampant qualitites of true bamboo. The small leaves have purplish autumn tones and the clusters of tiny white summer flowers give way to red berries in autumn. The popular dwarf form Nandina domestica 'Nana' grows to only*

about 40cm (16in) and has brilliant red and yellow tones in autumn.

Pyracantha (Firethorn) *There are many members of this group of spiny, evergreen shrubs. All require a sheltered site and a feature common to them is the showy display of red, orange or yellow fruits in autumn. Perhaps the best is Pyracantha fortuneana which carries red-to-crimson fruits from mid-autumn to late winter. They are hardy to all but the most ferocious of frosts.*

Raphiolepis (Indian hawthorn) *For an interesting effect in the garden the bluish-black fruits produced by the various species of Raphiolepis take some beating. These dense, evergreen shrubs make terrific informal hedges and a pleasing display of white flowers in spring is followed by the unusually coloured fruits in autumn. Raphiolepis indica, a very reliable species, will tolerate frosty and warmer areas alike.*

Schinus ariera (Peruvian pepper tree) *A beautiful ferny-foliaged evergreen tree growing 10-15m (30-45ft). It develops a sculptured, gnarled trunk and a spreading crown, and is fast growing with a weeping habit. It is wonderfully adaptable to different soils and climates; its drought tolerance makes it very popular in dry climates.*

Syzygium and Acmena (Lilly pilly) *There are a number of lilly pillies which are worth growing for the colourful fruits which can also be used to make delicious and unusual jam. Acmena smithii has white to pale mauve purple fruits in winter while Syzygium paniculatum has shiny rose-coloured ones in autumn. For contrast opt for the Syzygium coolminianum which provides unusual bluish berries in late autumn.*

The red berries of the deciduous *Cotoneaster horizontalis* provide a splash of autumn colour.

The Japanese flowering cherry tree
(*Prunus serrulata*) produces beautiful,
warm tones in autumn and spectacular
displays of white or pink spring blossoms.

Autumn Glory

Blazing displays for cooler months

After all the colourful flowers of spring and summer, autumn can seem like a let-down if you do not plan otherwise. The warm oranges, reds and yellows of the falling leaves of deciduous plants give just the right mood during the crisp, cool days of autumn.

The colour in these leaves arises from the fact that the green pigment chlorophyll (which normally dominates leaf colour) breaks down and allows other pigments to take over. Each deciduous species has its own special array of pigments for characteristic autumn tones. The trick is to choose the right deciduous tree or shrub for your district as some need colder weather than others to develop their most intense colours.

Parrotia persica

Buying deciduous trees and shrubs can be something of a lottery when it comes to getting the best in autumn colour. Many deciduous trees and shrubs are raised from seed and the resulting plants can vary in all sorts of characteristics, including the colour of the leaves during autumn.

Take your time when choosing autumn plants and make a short list of favourites and read up on them. In order to avoid disappointment, buy deciduous plants in autumn so what you see is what you get.

Deciduous trees tend to be much more tolerant of frost than other trees and shrubs. They shut down completely in winter and develop tough resting buds which can resist the slings and arrows of frost and even snow.

S. Kenny, Buskers End, Bowral NSW; M. Stowar

The Top Five

Deciduous Trees

Liquidambar styraciflua This large, majestic tree is perhaps one of the most reliable for spectacular colour over a wide range of climates. Be careful, however, as this tree will need more room to move than most and it is definitely not suitable for the average suburban block as it can play havoc with drains and foundations. If you do have an extra large block, an avenue planting of Liquidambars can be an awesome sight when in full autumn glory.

Sapium sebiferum
(Chinese tallow tree) *If you are looking for a small tree because your garden cannot accommodate large trees like the Liquidambar consider this colourful autumn gem. Growing to no more than 10m (32ft), it is extremely valuable as it colours well even in warmer climates. The range of colours produced is spectacular, from yellow to the deepest reds. It is also quite an adaptable tree as it can thrive in a variety of drainage conditions.*

Ginkgo biloba (Maidenhair tree)
This fascinating tree is considered to be a "living fossil" as its nearest relatives are known only from fossils from the Jurassic period (approximately 180 million years ago). It is a frost hardy tree with leaves not unlike a gigantic maidenhair fern. It can reach 15-25m (45-75ft) depending on growing conditions and develops golden-yellow autumn foliage.

Fraxinus species (Ash) *This is a large group of deciduous trees which originate in the northern hemisphere. All the species give some degree of autumn colour but some are much more spectacular than others. There are two varieties which really do stand out, however. The yellow or golden ash (Fraxinus excelsior 'Aurea') is a small tree (10-12m) which colours well over a wide range of climates. A feature of this tree is the sooty-black buds it forms on the end of the branches which contrast brilliantly with the golden-yellow autumn leaves. The claret ash (Fraxinus 'Raywood')is an Australian-raised variety which originated in South Australia and has achieved great popularity around the world because of its reliable autumn display of deep red foliage. A mixed planting of golden and claret ashes certainly makes for a stunning colour contrast. Reasonable drainage is all that is required to grow a good ash.*

Acer palmatum (Japanese maple)
This compact 4-5m (12-15ft) small, deciduous tree is indispensable for autumn colour with its yellow to scarlet tones. It is best grown in cool, humid climates with lots of mulch and summer water. There are many different cultivars of Japanese maple to choose from, featuring an enormous range of leaf shapes and colours. The cultivars must be grafted and are available from specialist nurseries.

The vibrant golden tones of the chestnut (*Castanea*) (1) add warmth to even a cool climate garden in autumn. Use varying colours of foliage to develop extra interest in a garden during the colder months with combinations such as this claret ash and liquidambar (2). The maple family (3) is particularly good at providing rich red autumnal tones, while the tulip tree (*Liriodendron tulipfera*) (4) provides glorious golden colour.

R. Hyett (1 & 4); J. Stowar (2); S. Kenny ; Buskers End, Bowral NSW (3)

The golden ash (*Fraxinus excelsior* 'Aurea') (1) is a popular choice for autumn colour. A huge tree, the copper beech (*Fagus sylvatica* 'Purpurea') (2) needs lots of room. The rich amber foliage of linden *(Tilia species)* (3) contrasts well with its dark trunk.

J. Stoavar (1); R. Hyett (2 & 3)

Bright Ideas for Autumn

Glorious Golds

Acer saccharinum (**Silver maple**)
Liriodendron tulipifera (**Tulip tree**)
Acer palmatum cvs. (**Japanese maple**)
Robinia pseudoacacia 'Frisia' (**False acacia**)
Koelreuteria paniculata (**Golden rain tree**)
Acer cappadocicum (**Caucasian maple**)
Acer platanoides (**Norway maple**)
Ginkgo biloba (**Maidenhair tree**)
Betula pendula (**Silver birch**)
Castanea sativa (**Sweet chestnut**)
Chimonanthus praecox (**Wintersweet**)
Populus nigra 'Italica' (**Lombardy poplar**)
Salix spp. (**Willow**)
Fraxinus excelsior 'Aurea' (**Golden ash**)

Shining Ambers and Oranges

Acer saccharum (**Sugar maple**)
Parrotia persica (**Persian ironwood**)
Diospyros kaki (**Chinese persimmon**)
Acer palmatum cvs especially
'Sango kaku' syn 'Senkaki'.
Prunus serrulata (**Flowering cherry**)
Lagerstroemia indica (**Crepe myrtle**)
Cornus spp (**Dogwood**)
Pistacia chinensis (**Chinese pistacia**)
Sapium sebiferum (**Chinese tallow tree**)

Glowing Reds

Acer rubrum (**Canadian maple**)
Acer x freemanii (**Lipstick tree**)
Acer palmatum cvs (**Japanese maple**)
Liquidambar styraciflua cvs
(**Liquidambar**)
Nyssa sylvatica (**Tupelo**)

Rich Reds

Fraxinus 'Raywood' (**Claret ash**)
Quercus palustris (**Pin oak**)
Quercus coccinea (**Scarlet oak**)
Acer palmatum (**Japanese maple**)
Acer japonicum 'Filicifolium'
(**Full moon maple**)
Liquidambar styraciflua 'Tirriki' 'Kia' and
'Burgundy' (**Liquidambar**)

Like many maples, the leaves of *Acer japonicum* (1) add a red glow to a garden. The silver maple (*Acer saccharinum*) is ideal for cooler climate gardens (2). The maidenhair tree (*Ginkgo biloba*) has yellow tones (3) while the Persian ironwood *(Parrotia persica)* has deep green leaves which turn to yellow, orange and a reddish-purple in autumn (4).

The Top Five

Evergreen Foliage Plants

Acacia baileyana (**Cootamundra wattle**) *One of the most popular species of Acacia with clusters of small, golden-yellow flowers which bloom in winter. The pollen-filled flowers attract birds and bees but can be a problem for asthma sufferers. This beautiful tree has arching branches and grows to around 6m (18ft) at a very swift rate so is ideal in situations where privacy is required or a space needs to be filled quickly.*

Acalypha wilkesiana (**Fijian fire plant or red hot cat's tail**) *This unusual evergreen shrub originates in Fiji and the surrounding islands and is suitable for warmer, tropical and sub-tropical climates. The foliage comes in a wide variety of colours from mid-green and yellow tones through to reddish bronze. Some varieties have multi-coloured leaves and the bright splash of colour they provide complements many other showy tropical ornamentals such as Bougainvilleas and poinsettias. This plant hates frost and does best in well-drained soils.*

Alternanthera dentata '**Rubiginosa**' *This evergreen perennial is very useful as a border plant, in warmer climates, as it only grows to about 50cm (20in) and the dark burgundy foliage can be used to create interesting contrasts. It responds well to clipping and can be easily divided for multiplication.*

Cotinus coggygria '**Purpurea**' (**Purple smoke bush**) *This beautiful purple foliaged plant is suitable for colder climates and should be grown in full sun to bring out the best colour in its rounded leaves. Its common name derives from the wispy clusters of tiny flowers which appear in summer. It is a plant which seems to have some ability to adapt and can be successfully grown in warm as well as cool climates.*

Eucalyptus species *A number of eucalypt species are prized for their wonderful blue-grey foliage. They have long been used as a backing foliage for cut flowers and there is no reason why you can't create a similar effect in your own garden. The soft, blue leaves are produced by many species of Eucalypts in the seedling stage and it is referred to as juvenile foliage. This juvenile display is lost as the tree ages and the familiar deep green sickle-shaped leaves take over.*

*However, there are a few eucalypts which retain the blue leaves for their whole life. The Argyle apple (*Eucalyptus cinerea*) forms a medium sized tree which grows to 15m (46ft) and tolerates frost and poor drainage. The silver-leafed mountain gum (E. *pulverulenta*) is perhaps the most spectacular of all Eucalypts and is highly prized in the cut flower trade. It usually forms a straggly, small tree, so the best way to grow it successfully is to prune regularly and hard, forcing the plant to grow as a compact shrub. The cider gum (E. *gunnii*) has been widely grown in England and Europe for its delicate, round, blue juvenile leaves. Originally from Tasmania, it performs best in colder climates where it will eventually form a medium-sized tree. A spectacular tree, you will need to allow lots of room for it to grow.*

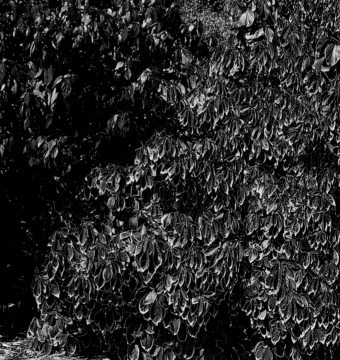

A. Stewart, Melbourne Botanic Gardens (1), Sydney Botanic Gardens (2); D. Harvey (5)

Evergreen Foliage Plants

It is not just deciduous plants that can provide unusual leaf colours. There are a number of plants which have interesting coloured foliage all year and this creates options for gardeners who are looking for particular colour effects and combinations.

The silvery-grey foliage of (*Eucalyptus cinerea*) (1) creates a spectacular shrub when clipped. The blue-grey leaves of the Spinning gum (*Eucalyptus perriniana) (2)* and the Silver gum *(Eucalyptus crenulata)* (3) are popular in floral arrangements because they highlight brighter colours. The Fijian fire plant *(Acalypha wilkesiana)* (4), a bushy shrub with oval, serrated leaves, is a vibrant addition to a garden. In fact, all varieties of Acalypha *(5)* provide a cheery burst of colour.

1 2

4

3

Variations on a Theme

Variegated plants are those in which the normal green leaf of a plant is combined with some other colour such as yellow, cream, red or orange. The great advantage of such plants is that they provide year-round colour and contrast, particularly during times when there are not many flowers. There is an extraordinary array of variegations in plants and they can sometimes provide very unusual effects in garden design. However, perhaps the best suggestion is to use them sparingly as too much variegated foliage tends to look rather unnatural.

Variegated forms are usually mutations which are propogated by cuttings or division and it is not difficult to find variegated forms of most ornamentals if you hunt around a little. Be careful though as the novelty of these unusual forms can look a bit overpowering if they are overused in the landscape.

The Top Five

Variegated Plants

Coleus blumei *Given its rapid growth, this popular soft-wooded perennial is normally grown from seed as an annual. It grows to about 0.5m (15in) and has multicoloured leaves with as many as four colours possible in the same leaf. The various forms of coleus are easily grown from cuttings and they will grow in full sun or semi-shade but will not tolerate frost.*

Hedera helix (Common English ivy)*Available in a bewildering array of variegated forms which can add interest to walls and fences. It does well in pots or can be used as a groundcover. It is a very vigorous climber which can be rather invasive, so be sure to give it a site where it will not get out of hand and overtake your garden.*

Phormium tenax (New Zealand flax) *This large clump-forming plant is extremely hardy and vigorous and its long linear, strap-like leaves make for interesting effects. The variegated plants range in colour from yellows to burgundy and orange tones with the colours being in the form of stripes along the length of the leaf. They range in height from 0.5 to 2m (15in to 6ft).*

Pittosporum eugenioides 'Variegatum' *An evergreen column-shaped small tree which is very popular in cultivation. This variety has a creamy coloured leaf margin that gives the whole plant a bright appearance. It is also an incredibly hardy plant which will tolerate quite heavy frosts*

Pittosporum tenuifolium 'James Stirling' *An outstanding small tree with small, rounded, silvery-green leaves with wavy edges. A subtle plant, it will blend easily with most plants in the garden. The light, silvery appearance is particularly useful in darker corners of the garden.*

The sword-shaped leaves of New Zealand flax (*Phormium* 'Sundowner') (1) make for a striking garden display. A colourful effect is achieved by mixing evergreen shrubs such as *Hebe* 'Veronica' with the bright blooms of Harlequin flower (*Sparaxis* 'tricolour') (2). Coleus (3) are ideally suited to subtropical areas or indoor conditions while Spanish bayonet (*Yucca aloifolia)* (4) prefers well-drained soil and full sun.

D. Drummond

If you are looking for an evergreen shrub or tree which could be used as a hedge or in topiary work you can't beat box *(Buxus).* This clipped variegated box is a classic example of the genus, which is popular with gardeners worldwide, and co-ordinates well with other plants.

Branching Out

Bark patterns and textures

One of the most under-rated sources of colour and texture in the garden is that provided by the barks of various trees and shrubs. Colourful barks can be used to complement or contrast with flowers growing in the garden or to provide a feature at a time of year when there may be a bit of a lull in the garden. The best sources of colour tend to be those trees which shed their bark every year revealing soft, shiny new bark underneath.

Deciduous shrubs such as the crepe myrtle (*Lagerstroemia indica*) and its many cultivars give some of the most striking effects as the bare, colourful trunks create dramatic and interesting effects through the winter when there may not be a lot of flowers in the garden. Crepe myrtles are very adaptable and frost hardy. They should be grown in full sun and will provide pastel-coloured flowers in summer and autumn, often followed by orange tones in their autumn foliage.

Silver birch (*Betula pendula*) is wonderful for cooler climates as the silvery-white bark is very striking during the winter. It also has

S. Kenny, Paradise Plants, Kulnura, NSW; A.Stewart

The unusual colours added by these lichens, above, are a bonus for Camellia lovers. The snow gum (*Eucalyptus pauciflora*), far left, develops fiery bark colours which are accentuated in cold climates. The paper bark maple (*Acer griseum*), left, makes a spectacular garden feature during its leafless period in winter.

1

good yellow leaf colour through the autumn and its weeping habit also helps make it a favourite tree in the right climate.

If you are looking for evergreen trees with interesting bark, then the eucalypts are worth considering. Trees such as the lemon-scented gum (*Eucalyptus citriodora*) have clear creamy-white bark which is clearly visible through the weeping, wispy foliage. The fresh lemon scent of the leaves is a another strong feature, especially after a shower of rain. It is an extremely adaptable tree which will tolerate a fair amount of frost. It does, however, prefer good drainage and a position in full sun. The Sydney red gum (*Angophora costata*) is similar in habit but has bold, bright orange bark and beautifully gnarled branches. The bark colour is especially intense in mid-summer just after the old bark has been shed. Once again this is a very adaptable tree as far as climate goes and it will grow quite as well in shallow soils as it does in its native sandstone-derived soil.

Silvery bark is a feature of a number of deciduous species including poplars and birches. The elegant lines and silver sheen of these poplar trunks, left, are emphasised by an underplanting of brillant buttercups (*Ranunculus* species). The smooth-barked apple tree or Sydney red gum (*Angophora costata*) (1) has a trunk which displays a gnarled appearance when grown near the coast. Green and orange lichens (2) form a colourful highlight on a tree trunk. The silver birch (*Betula pendula*) (3) has silver-white bark which turns rugged black as the tree ages. An orange lichen forms a coloured shroud around this tree trunk (4).

R. Hyett, Mernda Heights, Olinda Vic; A. Stewart (1)

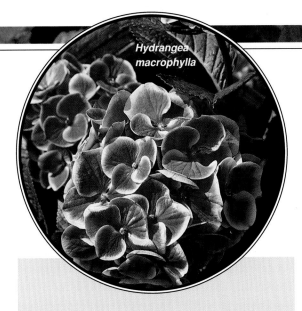

Hydrangea macrophylla

Hydrangea macrophylla

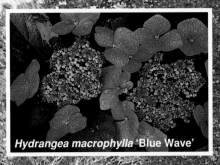

Hydrangea macrophylla 'Blue Wave'

Hydrangea macrophylla 'Blue Bonnet'

Hydrangea aborescens 'Grandiflora'

Hydrangea macrophylla Sibilla'

Hydrangea macrophylla

Adjusting Flower Colours

Pigments produced within petals provide the basis for flower colour and sometimes those pigments are influenced by the pH of the soil, that is, the acidity or alkalinity of the soil.

Hydrangeas are the perfect example of how soil pH affects plant colour. Many Hydrangea varieties will produce blue flowers in acid soils and pink flowers in alkaline soils.

However there are exceptions, such as the white-flowered varieties. White Hydrangeas do not have the blue or pink anthocyanin pigments so they they remain white regardless of the soil pH.

Altering the flower colourof Hydrangeas is a simple matter: iron sulphate or aluminium sulphate at a rate of 50-100grams per square metre (depending on the starting pH) will result in blue flowers, while garden lime at a rate of 50-300 grams per square metre (depending on the starting pH) will turn blues into purples and pinks.

Smaller intermittent doses will allow you to adjust the colour shade to your own liking. In each case sprinkle the fertiliser around the base of the plant and water in well. Keep the area well watered over the next few weeks to get the full benefit of your treatment.

S. Kenny, Moidart , Burradoo, NSW.   M.Stewart ; A. Stewart

82

Hydrangeas

Changing colours in your garden

The massed blooms of Hydrangeas bring to mind the warmer months and the bright light and colours associated with summer. But even after their prime, Hydrangeas continue to deliver interest as the blooms change from purple-blues and pinks through rich reds and burgundy tones until they dry and fade to brown. As the flowers become unsightly they should be pruned back. Cut each flower stem back about 30cm (1ft) to a healthy bud and remove the debris as it may harbour fungal diseases. Leave stems which have not flowered as they will produce next year's display.

Even as winter approaches, these Hydrangeas still create a colourful hedge which divides two levels of a rambling garden. The spent blooms can be pruned and used as indoor decorations.

Perfect Planning

Choosing the right plants for the job

Planning for colour in the garden begins with choosing the right plants for the job. Start by putting a plan down on paper, even if it is only a rough one. Use the chart at the back of this book as a reference to find not only the right colour but the right type of plant in terms of whether it is an annual or perennial, its height and width and so on. Then it is off to the local nursery to see if you can find the plants you want. Good retailers will be able to source some of the more unusual plants by ringing around the various wholesale nurseries which supply them.

In addition, make sure that you are getting value for money by choosing good quality plants. For annual seedlings beware of spindly looking plants which have been in the punnet too long. Even if the price is marked down, these sort of seedlings rarely recover to reach their proper potential. For bulbs look out for plump, firm

Bearded Iris and Centranthus are both long-lived perennials.

plants which are clean of any fungal growth. Trees and shrubs need to be checked to ensure a healthy root system. The ideal situation is healthy white roots just starting to poke out from the drainage holes. If you are in any doubt, especially if it is an expensive advanced specimen, ask the sales assistant to knock the plant out so you can see the root system. If the roots are curling around the inside of the pot, avoid the plant as it will become unstable as it increases in size in your garden. Clumpy perennials, such as Agapanthus tend to renew their root system regularly and being rootbound is not the problem it is with trees and shrubs.

Growing Healthy Plants

The key to creating a beautiful colour garden lies in following sound gardening principles. Firstly, take careful note of the growing information in the A to Z of Colourful Plants beginning on page 104. Having "green fingers" is all about matching up a plant's requirements for the right type of soil, watering and light levels – you don't have to learn these the hard way – many others have already done that before you! Another pitfall is grouping plants which have different requirements for light or water and the like. Try and gauge what sort of microclimate exists in each corner of your garden and then pick plants which suit not only the position but also the colour scheme you desire. There are a lot of questions to consider, so about now you will be starting to appreciate why good garden design is such an art form!

Anemones, left, grow from a bulb-like tuber. Here they frame a carpet of the ever-popular annual, Lobularia. This garden, below left, has been designed for a hot, dry climate. Hardy perennial sages in reds and purples provide a colourful foreground for an extensive planting of *Camellia sasanqua*, another hardy species.

should try and minimise the amount of water you use in the garden there are times when you must not skimp. Be sure to water plants freely during the week or two after transplanting them and also just before and during the flowering period. If plants suffer water stress during flowering it will often result in buds aborting and a general shortening of the overall flowering period.

Deadheading and Pruning

Pinching off dead flower heads (deadheading) can be a little time consuming, however, it often results in a much longer flowering period. This is particularly true for annuals which naturally die out after producing flowers and seeds. Pruning off dead flowers before they seed stimulates the plant to to produce more flowers to compensate for its lost flower babies. Deadheading will also help perennials and shrubs as they have similar tendencies. If you do not deadhead, the old flowers will rot off and the fungal organisms which cause this decay can then sometimes spread to the healthy flowers which are still on the plant.

Pruning to shape a plant should, as a rule, be done straight after flowering. Most species will follow flowering with a burst of growth. This means that by giving the plant a light trim back to a healthy bud you will encourage some nice bushy growth and set up a framework for the following year's flowering period.

Fertilising and Watering

As a general rule apply small amounts of fertiliser often during the growing season; this is generally the warmer months for trees and shrubs. Many bulbs, perennials and annuals grow quite actively through the winter so be observant and feed them if this is when they are active. Liquid fertilisers are readily available and, if you follow the manufacturer's directions, you shouldn't get into trouble with overfertilising. Remember, overfertilising can harm plants.

Placing a layer of compost or other organic material around the base of your plants, otherwise known as mulching, will help to preserve moisture. It will also, depending on the type of mulch used (e.g. rotted manure or home-made compost), release nutrients into the soil as it breaks down. While you

A Tropical Retreat

The rainforest garden is the perfect way to see the range of patterns and textures offered by green foliage. The lush lilly pilly leaves, the sword-shaped leaves of the gymea lily and the large fronds of the palm and tree ferns present a soothing green mass.

The serpentine mulched walk contains many Australian rainforest species which are noted for their unusual flowers and beautiful fruits and are suitable for frost-free areas. These provide a wonderful habitat for birds and animals. Many, such as the gymea lily, ivory curl flower and the umbrella tree, contain nectar while others like the lilly pilly and bangalow palm provide fruits to supplement the diet of their visitors.

A restful retreat from which to enjoy the garden and the wildlife can be found on a wooden bench nestled between the bangalow palms and native violets; stepping stones provide access from the path. From the wooden bench you can look out towards a bird bath which has been included to coax a range of birds into the garden. Clever path design and plantings of palms and ferns screen utility areas containing the garden shed and compost heap from the bench.

Tropical Concerns

Most of these plants prefer shady conditions so fast-growing "nurse" plants, such as wattles (Acacia species), are initially used to shelter ferns and palms until they become established. Then the "nurses" are removed. This garden will work best in heavier clay soils which retain more moisture. Copious amounts of compost dug into the soil and/or mulched around the top of the plants also helps. A network of mini sprinklers at the base of the plants will increase humidity during dry periods.

Key for Plan

Trees

Bangalow palm
(*Archontophoenix cunninghamiana*)

Umbrella tree
(*Schefflera actinophylla*)

Queensland firewheel tree
(*Stenocarpus sinuatus*)

Lilly pilly
(*Syzygium paniculatum*)

Shrubs

Small leaf lilly pilly
(*Acmena smithii var. minor*)

Ivory curl flower
(*Buckinghamia celsissima*)

Gymea lily
(*Doryanthes excelsa*)

Ferns

Birds nest fern
(*Asplenium australasicum*)

Soft tree fern
(*Dicksonia antarctica*)

Groundcovers

Matrush
(*Lomandra longifolia*)

Native violet
(*Viola hederacea*)

Red-hot favourites

❧

Sunny pinks for frosty areas

Allium giganteum
Aster novi-belgii
Camellia sasanqua cvs.
Canna x generalis
Centranthus ruber
Dahlia x hybrida
Echinachea purpurea
Erica darleyensis
Lavatera rosea
Oenothera speciosa rosea
Phlox paniculata
Sedum spectabile
Stachys byzantina

❧

Shady pinks for frosty areas

Anemone x hybrida
Astilbe tagetii
Bergenia cordifolia
Canna x generalis
Camellia japonica cvs.
Chorizema cordatum
Crowea exalta
Hydrangea macrophylla

❧

Shady pinks for frost-free areas

Anemone x hybrida
Camellia species varieties
Digitalis purpurea
Fuchsia varieties
Hippeastrum x hybrida
Impatiens walleriana and
New Guinea hybrids

❧

The Red Garden

A red garden is at once dramatic and powerful. Red is not for the lighthearted, it demands attention (and gets it). Reds with yellows produce a fiery result, while pale reds with soft mauves and blues are more calming. Strong reds often clash with strong blues but if that combination is your preference, then by all means use it. However, you may like to soften the planting with the inclusion of some purple-toned leaves so that the colours appear linked together.

Reds bring distance closer so if your garden is already tiny consider using the softer shades, say, pale salmon, silvery-pink or rose-pink of the group. Or, if your heart is set on red, make a real show of it and plant a bank of deep red flowers against glossy, green hedging. Try Camellias or rich, red roses.

Red flowers and foliage provide a nice surprise if planted around the bend in a pathway, or secreted away in a garden corner so they can't be seen immediately.

Don't be coerced by any well meaning neighbours or relatives who think red is vulgar, and yellow too gaudy. If they are the colours you want to have around you, then plant them, *but* give careful attention to the mood you want to create and the effect you want to achieve. If you want a restful haven in your garden, shocking vermillion and sunburst-yellow beds are not the way to go (blues and whites will be a better option), but if you want a welcoming entrance, a border of happy faced pansies in hues of yellow and orange might fit the bill perfectly.

A planting of foxgloves (*Digitalis*), above left, combines with perennial Phlox to create a beautiful feature. Asters, left, put on a rosy summer/autumn display, thrive in sunny conditions and will tolerate poor soils. A bank of dwarf red azaleas, right, are matched in tone by the red leaves of the Prunus trees to provide a pleasing result.

A Formal Pink Garden

This formal pink garden is designed for ease of movement as well as being a colourful retreat in a sunny, frost-free area. Entrance to the garden is via two wooden arbors adorned with climbers. The arbors are framed by a blueberry ash and a blireiana plum.

A stone bench, set back from the pathway, has behind it a planting of annuals against a backdrop of pink *Camellia sasanqua*, while a collection of daisies sits on each side of the bench. This area opens out onto a formal lawn which has as its focal point an urn overflowing with annuals.

An array of pink shrubs suitable for frost-free areas, including Hydrangea, Grevillea and tree in a hurry provides a screen near the pathway while a mass of smaller shrubs including roses, diosma and daisies shields the lawn. Perennials including Impatiens, daisies, lamb's ears, lilies, Erigeron and asters edge the lawn and path in shades of pink. A hedge of *Camellia japonica* ensures further privacy.

Key for Plan

Trees

Blueberry ash
(*Elaeocarpus reticulatus*)

Blireiana plum
(*Prunus x blireiana*)

Shrubs

Camellia japonica

Camellia sasanqua

Diosma
(*Coleonema pulchrum*)

Marguerite daisy
(*Argyranthemum* syn. *Chrysanthemum frutescens*)

Grevillea
(*Grevillea* 'Misty Pink')

Grevillea
(*Grevillea* 'Pink Surprise')

Hydrangea
(*Hydrangea macrophylla*)

Hybrid tea roses
(*Rosa* 'Ophelia')/(*Rosa* 'Perfume delight')

Tree in a hurry
(*Virgilia oroboides*)

Perennials

Belladonna lily/Nerine
(*Amaryllis belladonna*)/(*Nerine bowdenii*)

Dwarf New York aster
(*Aster novi-belgii*)

Erigeron
(*Erigeron karvinskianus*)

Impatiens/English daisy
(*Impatiens walleriana*)/(*Bellis perennis*)

Lamb's ears
(*Stachys byzantina*)

Groundcovers

Pink rock daisy
(*Brachycome* 'Pink Haze')

Annuals

Wallflower/ sweet william/stock/ primula/pansies
(*Cheiranthus cheiri*)/(*Dianthus barbatus*)
(*Matthiola incana*)/(*Primula malacoides*)/
(*Viola hybrids*)

Climbers

Sweet pea (*Lathyrus odoratus*)

Bower vine (*Pandorea jasminoides*)

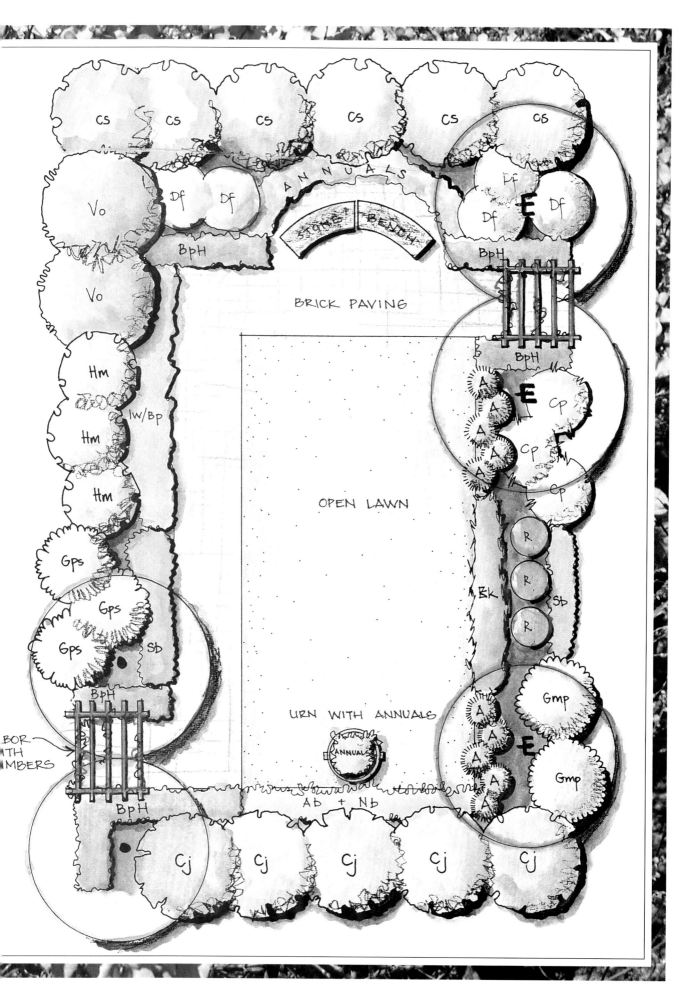

A Portable Grey Garden

Grey foliage is particularly resilient to tough environmental conditions so grey-foliaged plants are well suited to containers which have a tendency to dry out quickly. There is an enormous selection of plants available including shiny silvery-grey, heavily textured gun-metal grey or soft, grey-green. Terracotta troughs, bowls and planters provide adequate depth and space for root growth: they are also ideal for creating informal hedges and screens around an outdoor living area. With the exception of *Correa alba*, these plants are all suitable for frosty areas.

The daisy-like bright eyes *(Euryops pectinatus)* provide a wonderful splash of warm yellow from late autumn into winter. They are underplanted here with snow in summer *(Cerastium tomentosum)* which spills over the sides of the trough.

Many Australian indigenous species are well suited to containers because of their excellent drainage. Here the soft blue-grey foliage and white star-shaped flowers of a white Correa *(Correa alba)* are beautifully complemented by the earthy tones of a rounded terracotta pot.

French lavender *(Lavandula dentata)* with its fragrant purple spikes and silvery-grey foliage is perfect for pot culture. There are more than 25 varieties of lavender from which to choose with flower colours as diverse as white, pink, green and pale blue.

Many of the low-growing conifers do very well in pots, creating a cascade of tightly-bunched foliage. The purplish-grey of the Waukegan juniper *(Juniperus horizontalis* 'Douglassi') is a delight as a single planting or it could be combined with other taller conifer species.

One of the most hardy trees for container use is the European olive *(Olea europea* and cultivars). This tree has been standardised to encourage dense growth and underplanted with lamb's ears *(Stachys byzantina)*. The lamb's ears soften the edge and serve to emphasise the formal shape of the olive tree.

The White Garden

The white garden is the essence of simplicity, freshness and tranquillity. What could be more appealing that a curtain of white Wisteria, a carpet of alyssum, rows of luminous Gardenia, drifts of paper white hyacinths or creamy old roses.

It's hard to go wrong with white. It complements every house colour and white gardens really come into their own in soft light, so they look especially good at sunrise and sunset, and they absolutely shine in moonlight.

White flowers are best matched with grey and silver foliage or pastel hues to tone down their dazzling whiteness.

Pale and interesting

Sunny whites for frosty areas

Cistus spp.
Convolvulus cneorum
Gaura lindheimeri
Lychnis coronaria
Magnolia denudata
Philadelphus spp.
Romneya coulteri
Viburnum spp.
Zephyranthes candida

Shady whites for frosty areas

Anemone x hybrida
Camellia japonica
Correa alba
Polygonatumn x hybridum
Prostanthera cuneata
Rhododendron azalea 'Alba'
Zantedeschia aethiopica

Sunny whites for frost-free areas

Brachycome multifida
Chamelaucium uncinatum
Gypsophila paniculata
Grevillea 'Moonlight'
Murraya paniculata
Pandorea jasminoides

Create a pretty corner in spring with masses of white tulips, above, surrounded by pansies. Another idea is to plant masses of white lavender, right, set here against a background of pine.

A White Courtyard

A southerly aspect, or a shaded garden can be highlighted with an array of white flowers. These situations often produce moist conditions with limited light. The courtyard in this example is simply planted with a formal arrangement of white flowering species suitable for frost-free areas.

The gentle sound of tricking water is generated by a feature wall fountain. This is framed by two clipped Camellias. In front of these a collection of arum lilies provide a delicate scent while a small hedge of white Impatiens lies underneath the wall fountain. Erigeron gently spills over the edge of the garden creating a delicate effect.

Other potted species include a star jasmine trained on a wire frame, native violets and a standard Hill's weeping fig is underplanted with mondo grass.

Key for Plan

 Standard Hill's weeping fig *(Ficus microcarpa var. hillii)*

 White Camellia *(Camellia japonica)*

 Arum lily *(Zantedeschia aethiopica)*

 Star jasmine *(Trachelospermum jasminoides)*

 Mondo grass *(Ophiopogon japonicus)*

 Native violet *(Viola hederacea)*

 Impatiens *(Impatiens walleriana)*

 Erigeron *(Erigeron mucronatus)*

Blue moods

❧

Sunny blues for frosty areas

Allium giganteum
Aster novi-belgii
Camellia sasangua cvs.
Canna x generalis
Centranthus ruber
Dahlia x hybrida
Echinachea purpurea
Erica darleyensis
Lavatera rosea
Oenothera speciosa rosea
Phlox paniculata
Stachys byzantina
Sedum spectabile

❧

Shady blues for frosty areas

Anemone x hybrida
Astilbe tagetii
Bergenia cordifolia
Camellia japonica cvs.
Canna x generalis
Chorizema cordatum
Crowea exalta
Hydrangea macrophylla

❧

Sunny blues for frost-free areas

Alpina caerulea
Agapanthus praecox
Dianella revoluta
Elaeocarpus reticulatus
Hydrangea hispanica
Hydrangea macrophylla

❧

The mauve *Brachycome multifida*, left, blends with the blue of forget-me-not (*Myosotis*). *Lavandula* 'Munstead', above left, is highly fragrant with deep blue-purple flowers. This purple *Salvia*, above right, is a long-lived and compact perennial. Spanish bluebells, above, (*Hyacinthoides*) are bulbs which naturalise in the garden. A popular annual, Larkspur (*Consolida ambigua*), opposite, provides classic blue and pastel shades for spring display.

The Blue Garden

C̲ool blues and mauves are synonymous with calm, serenity and reserve; for most of us blue recalls the long days of summer – clear skies and azure water.

However, blue is a lot more than simply azure, the flowers in this spectrum run from ice blue to indigo, from deepest violet to powdery purple, from pale turquoise to steely lavender.

Rarely are blue flowers all blue. Often the petals are paler at the edges and darker in the centre, and many have centres of a contrasting colour, for example the alpine aster and blue potato vine have yellow centres while the pincushion flower has a white, fluffy centre.

Blues tend to enlarge an area, so if you want a narrow space to look wider, plant blues and mauves, perhaps interspersed with grey or green foliage. If you want your garden to look bigger, plant blues along your boundary fence. Borders of catmint or lavender along a pathway will appear to increase the length of the walkway.

Combining blues with yellows will make the yellows seem even brighter, and blues coupled with reds will make the reds appear even richer. A touch of contrasting white will heighten the colour of the blues and make the whites appear very clean, and blue with green is always a winner.

A Sunny Blue Garden

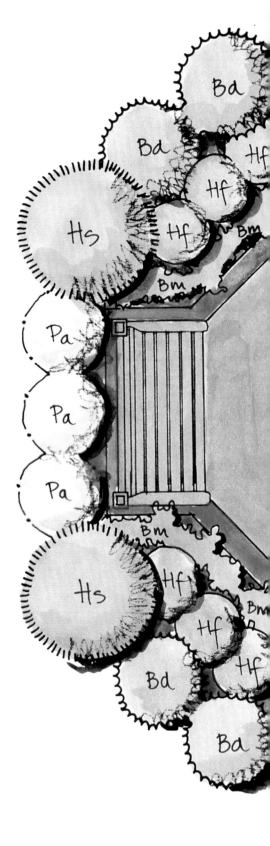

A sunny haven in the garden can be enhanced with a selection of plants in cooling blue tones. Designed to flower throughout the year, this private blue garden with a selection of plants for frost-free areas will provide a great place to relax. The entrance is framed with a canopy of Jacarandas underplanted with blue Agapanthus, French lavender and willmott blue. A series of groundcovers including rock daisies, catmint and sweet violets, encircle the pathways and provide gentle perfumes and a range of blue and purple highlights.

Screening the garden is a selection of shrubs with varying foliage and flowers including Plumbago, Syrian Hibiscus, Hebes, Hydrangea and the sweetly scented butterfly bush. A sandstone column with a brass sundial creates a focal point. This feature is surrounded by the delicate blue Felicia daisies and the greenish foliage of the wild mint. A timber bench provides a great place to enjoy the sunshine and the range of pretty blues.

Key for Plan

Trees

 Jacaranda
(Jacaranda mimosifolia)

Shrubs

 Butterfly bush
(Buddleia davidii)

Willmott blue
(Ceratostigma willmottianum)

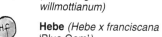

Hebe *(Hebe x franciscana 'Blue Gem')*

Syrian hibiscus *(Hibiscus syriacus)*

Hydrangea
(Hydrangea macrophylla)

French lavender
(Lavandula dentata)

Plumbago
(Plumbago auriculata)

Groundcovers

 Blue agapanthus
(Agapanthus orientalis)

 Wild mint *(Ajuga reptans)*

 Rock daisy *(Brachycome multifida)*

 Catmint *(Nepeta x faassenii)*

 Sweet violet *(Viola odorata)*

 Blue daisy *(Felicia amelloides)*

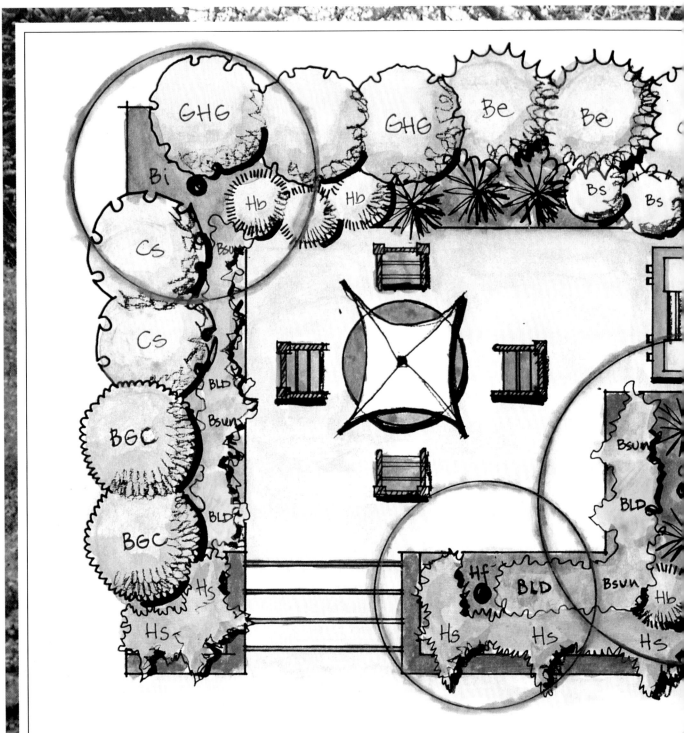

Key for Plan

Trees

Coastal banksia
(*Banksia integrifolia*)

Silky oak
(*Grevillea robusta*)

Native frangipani
(*Hymenosporum flavum*)

Shrubs

Heath banksia
(*Banksia ericifolia*)

Giant candles banksia
(*Banksia* 'Giant Candles')

Yellow bottlebrush
(*Callistemon salignus*)

Grevillea
(*Grevillea* 'Honey Gem')

Grevillea
(*Grevillea* 'Sandra Gordon')

Shrubs

Hairpin banksia
(*Banksia spinulosa*)

Golden kangaroo paw
(*Anigozanthos* 'Bush Gems')

Paper daisy
(*Helichrysum bracteatum*)

A Golden Terrace

This outdoor living area is designed for people who live in frost-free areas and enjoy al fresco entertaining all year round. Many of the Australian species featured including Banksias, Grevilleas and Callistemons put on their best displays in winter and so provide a touch of colour during the chilly months. The plants chosen for this garden are suitable for frost-free areas. Here they have been used as screening plants to create a secluded space. Softening the edge of the garden is a selection of yellow rock daisy cultivars including 'Sunburst' and 'Lemon Drops'. The golden blooms of a Guinea flower cascade over a small retaining wall while smaller shrubs such as hairpin Banksia, golden kangaroo paw and paper daisies attract birdlife to the garden. Other native trees including a coastal Banksia, silky oak and a native frangipani provide a cooling canopy for hot summer days.

Groundcovers

 Rock daisy 'Lemon Drops'
(*Brachycome* 'Lemon Drops')

 Rock daisy 'Sunburst'
(*Brachycome* 'Sunburst')

 Climbing guinea flower
(*Hibbertia Scandens*)

The Yellow Garden

The yellow garden is just bursting with warmth and happiness, it is the colour we see best in daylight. Spring is heralded by the arrival of yellow – daffodils, crocus, tulips – such a great tonic after the darkness and cold of winter.

From pale lemon to glowing yellow, from rich butter to brillant gold, yellow seems to sparkle, always adding a touch of vibrancy.

Borders of marigolds, an arbour of tiny yellow Banksia roses, a walkway of Laburnum, beds of buttercups or an avenue of wattles can't help but lift your spirits.

Warm colours tend to decrease the size of an area, so if you want your garden to look cozier, plant borders of bright yellow, orange and red. A dynamic effect is guaranteed. Alternatively, pale yellow or soft gold can extend the scale of the area, appearing to push back the boundaries.

Yellow is perfect paired with blues and mauves – opposites on the colour wheel – and with white and green.

A yellow Rhododendron adds vibrant colour and rich, spicy fragrance, top left; it makes a strong statement paired with yellow primula. A hardy perennial, nasturtiums (*Tropaeolum*), left, are a bright groundcover for sunny gardens. Massed yellow and white flowers,right, can make a dramatic impact. Here a row of yellow pansies (*Viola x wittrockiana*) is teamed with white Chrysanthemums and a yellow backdrop of buttercups (*Ranunculus asiaticus*).

B. Wilson; D. Harvey

Glow of gold

❧

Sunny golds for frosty areas

Acer japonica 'Aurea'
Chimonanthus praecox
Euphorbia spp.
Euryops pectinatus
Griselina littoralis
   'Variegata'
Hamamelis mollis
Helichrysum bracteatum
Hemerocallis sp.
Hibbertia scandens
Hypericum spp.
Iris x germanica
Iris pseudacorus
Kerria japonica
Senecio cineraria
Rosa spp.
Rudbeckia fulgida
Tropaeolum majus
   'Mutabilis'

❧

Shady golds for frosty areas

Aucuba japonica 'Aurea'
Dietes bicolor
Elaeagnus pungens
   'Maculata'
Euonymus japonicus
   'Variegata'
Helichrysum petiolare
   'Limeglow'
Hibbertia scandens
Lysimachia nummularia
   'Aurea'
Mahonia aquifolium

❧

Shady golds for frost-free areas

Allamanda cathartica
Aucuba japonica
Backhousia citriodora
Codiaeum variegatum
Euonymus japonicus
Hibbertia dentata
Impatiens repens

❧

A to Z of Colourful Plants

T his chart is designed to help you select plants which will be suitable for your garden. Not every plant mentioned will be easily found in retail outlets in every area. However, it will often be possible to track down the more obscure plants through mail order nurseries which advertise in specialist gardening magazines from your local newsagent.

We have concentrated mostly on plants suitable for Mediterranean, temperate and subtropical areas, which covers most readers. However, if you live in arid or desert areas you will find many of the plants for Mediterranean climates worth trying. Similarly for tropical areas, plants recommended for subtropical and warm temperate areas will adapt to some extent to the tropics.

Here are some explanations of the terms used in the table to help you use it.

WARM TEMPERATE CLIMATES – temperatures rarely, if ever, below freezing.

COOL TEMPERATE CLIMATES – mild (0° to -5°C) severe frosts (-5° to -15°C) experienced every winter.

FROST TENDER – damage will be caused by any frost.

MODERATELY OR MILDLY FROST HARDY – plants will tolerate light frosts without significant damage.

FROST HARDY – plants will tolerate frosts to -5°C without significant damage.

VERY FROST HARDY – plants will tolerate frosts to -10°C without significant damage.

GOOD DRAINAGE – when a hole is filled with water it drains within minutes.

MODERATE DRAINAGE – when a hole is filled with water it drains within hours.

POOR DRAINAGE – when a hole is filled with water it drains within days.

by Angus Stewart

Botanic name	Common name	Family	Height x width
Acacia baileyana	Cootamundra wattle	Mimosaceae	6-10x5m (20-30x15ft)
Acacia podalyriifolia	Queensland silver wattle	Mimosaceae	5x3-4 (15x9-12)
Acalypha wilkesiana	Fijian fire plant	Euphorbiaceae	2.5x2.5 (8x8)
Acanthus mollis	Oyster plant	Acanthaceae	1x1 (3x3)
Acer cappadocimum	Causican maple	Aceraceae	20-25x5-8 (60-75x15-25)
Acer griseum	Paperbark maple	Aceraceae	6-8x3 (18-25x10)
Acer japonicum 'Aureum'	Golden maple	Aceraceae	2.5x2 (8x6)
Acer japonicum 'Filicifolium'	Full moon maple	Aceraceae	4x2 (12x6)
Acer palmatum	Japanese maple	Aceraceae	4-5x3-4 (12-15x9-12)
Acer platanoides	Norway maple	Aceraceae	15-20x10 (45-60x30)
Acer rubrum	Red maple	Aceraceae	15-20x5 (45-60x15)
Acer saccharinum	Silver maple	Aceraceae	30x10 (90x30)
Acer saccharum	Sugar maple	Aceraceae	12-15x5 (36-45x15)
Acmena smithii	Creek lilly pilly	Myrtaceae	8-10 (24x30)
Agapanthus praecox (synonym orientalis)	Agapanthus	Liliaceae	1x0.6 (3x2)
Ageratum houstonianum	Floss flower	Asteraceae	0.3x0.3 (1x1)
Ajuga reptans 'Jungle Beauty'	Bugle flower	Lamiaceae	0.3x0.6 (1x2)
Alcaea rosea	Hollyhock	Malvaceae	1.5-2x0.6 (4-6x1)
Alternanthera dentata 'Rubiginosa'	Alternanthera	Amaranthaceae	0.5x indefinite (2x indefinite)
Amaryllis belladonna	Belladonna lily	Amaryllidaceae	1x0.5 (3x1.5)
Anemone x hybrida	Japanese windflower	Ranunculaceae	0.6-1 (2x3)
Angophora costata	Sydney red gum	Myrtaceae	15-25x10 (45-75x30)
Anigozanthos 'Bush Dawn'	Kangaroo paw	Haemodoraceae	2x1 (6x3)
Anigozanthos 'Bush Gold'	Kangaroo paw	Haemodoraceae	1x0.5 (3x1.5)

Plant type	Flower colour	Flowering time	Colourful features	Preferred climate & growing notes & special uses
evergreen tree	bright yellow	mid winter	flowers & grey feathery foliage	Cool temperate to warm temperate, full sun, moderate drainage, moderately frost hardy. Self-seeds readily and can invade bushland areas.
evergreen shrub to small tree	bright yellow	early winter	flowers & grey foliage	Cool temperate to warm temperate, full sun, moderate drainage, moderately frost hardy. Self-seeds readily and can invade bushland areas.
evergreen shrub	dull red	summer	foliage & flowers	Warm temperate to subtropical, full to part sun, good drainage, frost tender. Many varieties featuring different leaf colours & patterns.
evergreen soft-wood perennial	mauve & white	late spring	glossy green foliage & flowers	Cold continental, cool to warm temperate, full to part sun, good drainage, very frost hardy.
deciduous tree	greenish-yellow	spring	autumn foliage orange to red	Mediterranean to cool temperate, full sun, good drainage, very frost hardy.
deciduous tree	greenish-yellow	spring	autumn foliage orange to red	Cool temperate, full sun, good drainage, very frost hardy.
deciduous tree	purplish-red	spring	foliage is golden through the growing season	Mediterranean to cool temperate, full sun, good drainage, very frost hardy.
deciduous tree	purplish-red	spring	autumn foliage orange to red	Mediterranean to cool temperate, full sun, good drainage, very frost hardy. Unusual fine leaf form.
deciduous small tree	cream	spring	autumn foliage	Cool to warm temperate, full to part sun, good drainage, frost hardy. Numerous grafted varieties such as 'Sango kaku' & 'Senkaki' available which have special foliage colours.
deciduous tree	greenish-yellow	spring	autumn foliage	Cool temperate, full to part sun, good drainage, frost hardy. The variety 'Crimson King' has reddish crimson leaves right through the growing season.
deciduous tree	reddish	spring	autumn foliage orange to scarlet	Cool temperate, full to part sun, good drainage, frost hardy.
deciduous tree	greenish-yellow	spring	autumn foliage bright yellow	Cool temperate, full to part sun, good drainage, frost hardy.
deciduous tree	yellow	spring	autumn foliage bright golden to red	Cool temperate, full to part sun, good drainage, frost hardy.
evergreen small tree	white	summer	flowers & white to mauve fruits	Warm temperate to subtropical, full to part sun, good drainage, frost tender. Fruits are edible. Great screen plant, compact varieties available.
clumping evergreen perennial	blue or white	summer	flowers	Mediterranean, cool to warm temperate, full to part sun, moderate drainage, moderately frost hardy. Good cut flower or pot plant.
annual	mauve or white	summer to autumn	flowers	Mediterranean, cool to warm temperate, full to part sun, good drainage, moderately frost tolerant. Deadhead regularly for longer flowering display.
groundcovering soft-wood perennial	blue	spring	purplish leaves & flowers	Mediterranean, cool to warm temperate, full to part sun, moderate drainage, very frost tolerant.
biennial	pink yellow cream	summer to autumn	flowers	Mediterranean, cool to warm temperate, full sun, good drainage, very frost hardy. Staking flower stems is a good idea.
soft-wood perennial	n/a	n/a	foliage is always red	Warm temperate to subtropical, full to part sun, good drainage, frost tender. Clip regularly to maintain compact habit.
deciduous bulb	pink or white	autumn	flowers	Mediterranean, cool to warm temperate, full sun, moderate drainage, frost hardy. Good cut flower.
herbaceous perennial	pink or white	autumn	flowers	Cool to warm temperate, part sun, good drainage, frost hardy. Suckers and spreads to form large clumps.
evergreen tree	white	summer	flowers & red bark	Cool to warm temperate, full sun, good drainage, moderately frost hardy. Bark peels in summer revealing spectacular red new bark underneath.
evergreen soft-wood perennial	yellow	spring	flowers	Mediterranean, cool to warm temperate, full sun, perfect drainage, moderately frost hardy. Cut back old flower stems to the base.
evergreen soft-wood perennial	yellow	all year	flowers	Mediterranean, cool to warm temperate, full sun, perfect drainage, moderately frost hardy. Cut back old flower stems to the base.

Botanic name	Common name	Family	Height x width	Plant type	Flower colour	Flowering time
Anigozanthos 'Bush Ranger'	Kangaroo paw	Haemodoraceae	0.6x0.3m (2x1ft)	soft-wood perennial	red	all year
Antirrhinum majus	Snapdragon	Scrophulariaceae	0.2-1x0.2-0.5 (1-3x1-2)	perennial grown as an annual	all except blue & black	spring to autumn
Arbutus unedo	Irish strawberry tree	Ericaceae	8x8 (25x25)	evergreen tree	white	autumn winter
Archontophoenix cunninghamiana	Bangalow palm	Arecaceae	20x5 (60x15)	evergreen tree (palm)	mauve	summer
Arctotis x hybrida	African daisy	Asteraceae	0.5x0.5 (1.5x1.5)	soft-wood perennial	white, pink, red, yellow, orange	winter to summer
Argyranthemum (syn. *Chrysanthemum*) *frutescens*	Marguerite daisy	Asteraceae	1x1 (3x3)	soft-wood perennial	pink or white	spring to autumn
Asplenium australasicum	Birds nest fern	Aspleniaceae	0.5-1x1 (2-3x3)	fern	n/a	n/a
Aster novi-belgii	New York aster	Asteraceae	1.2x0.5 (4x2)	herbaceous perennial	white or pink or red	autumn
Babiana stricta	Baboon flower	Iridaceae	0.3x0.3 (1x1)	deciduous corm	purple-blue	spring
Banksia 'Giant Candles'	Banksia	Proteaceae	4x3 (12x9)	evergreen shrub	orange	late autumn winter
Banksia integrifolia	Coastal banksia	Proteaceae	15x5 (45x15)	evergreen tree	yellow	winter
Begonia x tuberhybrida	Tuberous begonia	Begoniaceae	0.6-0.9x0.3 (2-3x1)	perennial forming a tuber	yellow, orange, pink, red	summer
Berberis thunbergii 'Atropurpurea'	Barberry	Berberidaceae	1-1.5x3 (3-5x9)	deciduous shrub	yellow	spring
Berberis rubrostyla	Barberry	Berberidaceae	1.5x1.5 (5x5)	deciduous shrub	pinkish white	spring
Bergenia cordifolia	Bergenia	Saxifragaceae	0.5x0.6 (1.5-2)	soft-wood perennial	pink	winter-spring
Betula pendula	Silver birch	Betulaceae	20x10 (60x30)	deciduous tree	yellow-green	spring
Bougainvillea x buttiana	Bougainvillea	Nyctaginaceae	depends on support	evergreen climber	various	summer to autumn
Brachycome 'Sunburst' & 'Lemon Drops'	Brachycome daisy	Asteraceae	0.3x1 (1x3)	soft-wood perennial	yellow	spring to autumn
Brachycome 'Pink Haze'	Brachycome daisy	Asteraceae	0.3x1 (1x3)	soft-wood perennial	soft pink	all year
Brunfelsia bonodora (syn. *latifolia*)	Yesterday, today & tomorrow	Solanaceae	1.5-2x2 (4-6x6)	evergreen shrub	blue fading to white	late winter-spring
Buckinghamia celsissima	Ivory curl flower	Proteaceae	3x2 (9x6)	evergreen shrub	white	late spring
Buddleia davidii	Butterfly bush	Buddleiaceae	5x3 (15x9)	deciduous shrub	lilac	mid-summer to autumn

Colourful features	Preferred climate & growing notes & special uses
flowers	Mediterranean, cool to warm temperate, full sun, perfect drainage, moderately frost hardy. Cut back old flower stems to the base.
flowers	Mediterranean, cool to warm temperate, full sun, good drainage, moderately frost hardy. Many different varieties available in a range of heights and colours.
flowers & reddish-orange fruits	Cool to warm temperate, full sun, good drainage, frost hardy. Fascinating fruits.
glossy foliage & flowers & fruits	Warm temperate to subtropical, full sun, good drainage, frost tender. Reliable palm species.
flowers	Warm temperate to subtropical, full sun, good drainage, frost tender. Good for coastal areas.
flowers	Mediterranean, cool to warm temperate, full sun, good drainage, moderately frost hardy. Deadhead regularly for longer flowering. Federation daisies include a range of new varieties such as 'Surprise Party' and 'Summer Angel'.
glossy broad foliage	Warm temperate to subtropical, shady position, good drainage, frost tender.
flowers	Mediterranean, cool to warm temperate, full to part sun, frost hardy. Great cut flower.
flowers	Mediterranean, cool to warm temperate, full to part sun, good drainage, frost tender. Excellent as a pot plant.
flowers	Cool to warm temperate to subtropical, full sun, good drainage, moderately frost hardy. Good for attracting birds.
flowers	Cool to warm temperate to subtropical, full sun, good drainage, moderately frost hardy. Good for attracting birds. Great for seaside areas.
flowers	Warm temperate to subtropical, shady position, good drainage, very frost tender. Mainly grown as a potted specimen.
flowers & purple leaves, red fruits	Cold continental to cool temperate, full sun, good drainage, frost hardy.
flowers & bright red fruits	Cold continental to cool temperate, full sun, good drainage, very frost hardy.
flowers & bold dark green foliage	Cool to warm temperate, full to part sun, good drainage, frost hardy.
silvery bark & yellow autumn foliage	Cold continental to cool temperate, full sun, good drainage, frost hardy.
flowers	Warm temperate to subtropical, full sun, good drainage, frost tender. Feed and prune only after flowering.
flowers	Cool to warm temperate, full sun, good drainage, frost tender. Prune back after each flush of flowers.
flowers	Cool to warm temperate, full sun, good drainage, frost tender. Prune back after each flush of flowers.
flowers	Warm temperate to subtropical, full to part sun, good drainage, frost tender. Prune lightly after flowering.
flowers	Warm temperate to subtropical, full to part sun, good drainage, frost tender. Very free flowering and spectacular in warm climates
flowers & white-backed leaves	Cold continental to cool temperate, full sun, good drainage, very frost hardy. Prune heavily after flowering for compact habit.

Begonia x tuberhybrida

Arctotis x hybrida

Brunfelsia bonodora

R. Hyett

107

Camellia sasanqua

Cordyline

Cineraria x hybrida

D. Harvey; S. Kenny

Botanic name	Common name	Family	Height x width (m)
Buxus sempervirens	Box	Buxaceae	5x5m (15x15ft)
Callistemon 'White Anzac'	Bottlebrush	Myrtaceae	1.5x2 (5x6)
Callistemon pinifolius	Bottlebrush	Myrtaceae	1.5x1.5 (5x5)
Callistemon salignus	Willow bottlebrush	Myrtaceae	8-10x 5 (25-30x15)
Calocephalus brownii	Cushion bush	Asteraceae	0.5x0.5 (2x2)
Camellia sasanqua 'Little Liane'	Camellia	Theaceae	2x1 (6x3)
Camellia sasanqua 'Paradise Petite'	Camellia	Theaceae	2x1 (6x3)
Canna x generalis 'Rubrum'	Canna lily	Cannaceae	2x2 (6x6)
Castanea sativa	Sweet chestnut	Fagaceae	15x5 (45x15)
Centranthus ruber	Centranthus	Valerianaceae	0.6-1x0.5-0.6 (2-3x2)
Cerastium tomentosum	Snow in summer	Caryophyllaceae	0.1x1 (0.3x3)
Ceratopetalum gummiferum	New South Wales Christmas bush	Cunoniaceae	5x2 (15x6)
Ceratostigma willmottianum	Willmott blue	Plumbaginaceae	0.75x0.75 (2.5 x 2.5)
Chimonanthus praecox	Wintersweet	Calycanthaceae	2.5x3 (8x10)
Chorizema cordatum	Flame pea	Fabaceae	0.8x1.5 (3x5)
Cineraria cruenta syn. *Senecio x hybrida*	Cineraria	Asteraceae	0.5x0.5 (1.5x1.5)
Citrus aurantifolia	Lime	Rutaceae	5x3 (15x9)
Clivia miniata	Clivia	Amaryllidaceae	0.5x0.6 (1.5x 2)
Coleonema pulchrum 'Sunset Gold'	Golden diosma	Rutaceae	1x1 (3x3)
Coleus blumei	Coleus	Lamiaceae	0.5x0.3 (1.5x1)
Cordyline rubra	Cordyline	Agavaceae	3x1-2 (9x3-6)
Cordyline stricta	Cordyline	Agavaceae	2-4x1-2 (6-12x3-6)

Plant type	Flower colour	Flowering time	Colourful features	Preferred climate & growing notes & special uses
evergreen shrub	n/a	n/a	glossy dark green foliage	Cool to warm temperate, full sun, good drainage, frost hardy. Great for hedges and screens.
evergreen shrub	white	spring & autumn	flowers	Cool to warm temperate, full sun, tolerates poor drainage, frost hardy. Prune back old flowers after flowering.
evergreen shrub	green	summer to autumn	flowers	Cool to warm temperate, full sun, tolerates poor drainage, frost hardy. Prune back past old flowers after flowering. Good for attracting birds.
evergreen tree	yellow or red	summer to autumn	flowers & pinkish-red new growth	Cool to warm temperate, full sun, tolerates poor drainage, frost hardy. Prune back past old flowers after flowering. Good for attracting birds.
soft-wood perennial	yellowish-white	summer	silver foliage & flowers	Cool to warm temperate, full sun, good drainage, frost hardy. Spectacular foliage plant.
evergreen shrub	pinkish-white	autumn	flowers & glossy dark green foliage	Mediterranean, cool to warm temperate, full to part sun, good drainage, frost hardy. Fantastic plant for topiary or hedges.
evergreen shrub	soft pink	autumn	flowers & glossy dark green foliage	Mediterranean, cool to warm temperate, full to part sun, good drainage, frost hardy. Fantastic plant for topiary or hedges.
clumping soft-wood perennial	orange	summer	flowers & maroon foliage	Warm temperate to subtropical, full to part sun, tolerates poor drainage, frost tender. Forms large clumps if allowed.
deciduous tree	yellow	spring	yellow autumn foliage	Cold continental to cool temperate, full to part sun, good drainage, very frost hardy.
clumping perennial	red or white	spring to autumn	flowers	Mediterranean to cool temperate, full sun, good drainage, frost hardy. Self-seeds and tolerates poor soils.
soft-wood perennial	white	spring & summer	flowers & grey foliage	Mediterranean, cool to warm temperate, full sun, very frost hardy. Great for covering banks or other exposed areas.
evergreen shrub	white ageing to red	early summer	flowers	Cool to warm temperate, full to part sun, moderately frost hardy. Wonderful cut flower. Prune straight after flowering.
deciduous shrub	blue	summer to autumn	flowers fruits & autumn foliage	Mediterranean, cool to warm temperate, full sun, good drainage, frost hardy.
deciduous shrub	yellow	winter	flowers	Mediterranean, cool to warm temperate, full sun, good drainage, moderately frost hardy. Exquisite fragrance.
evergreen shrub	orange and pink	spring	flowers	Mediterranean, cool to warm temperate, full to part sun, good drainage, frost tender.
perennial grown as an annual	blue, red, pink or white	winter to spring	flowers	Cool to warm temperate, full to part sun, good drainage, mildly frost tolerant.
evergreen tree	white	winter	flowers & greenish-yellow fruits	Cool to warm temperate, full sun, good drainage, frost tender. Great in a pot.
soft-wood clumping perennial	orange or yellow	autumn or spring	flowers & dark green foliage	Warm temperate to subtropical, part sun to deep shade, good drainage, frost tender. Excellent for growing at the base of trees.
evergreen shrub	pink	spring	flowers & golden foliage	Mediterranean, cool to warm temperate, good drainage, mildly frost hardy.
perennial grown as an annual	mauve	summer	brightly coloured foliage & flowers	Warm temperate to subtropical, full to part sun, good drainage, frost tender. Many different varieties with varying colours and shapes.
perennial shrub	mauve & white	summer	flowers & bright red fruits in late summer-autumn	Warm temperate to subtropical, full sun, good drainage, frost tender. Interesting strap-like foliage.
perennial shrub	white or pink	summer	flowers & purplish fruits in late summer-autumn	Warm temperate to subtropical, full sun, good drainage, frost tender. Interesting strap-like foliage.

Botanic name	Common name	Family	Height x width	Plant type	Flower colour	Flowering time
Cornus florida 'Alba'	Flowering dogwood	Cornaceae	5-8x5-8m (15-25ft)	deciduous tree	pinkish-white	spring
Cornus kousa 'Chinensis'	Dogwood	Cornaceae	7x5 (20x15)	deciduous shrub to small tree	white	spring
Correa alba	White correa	Rutaceae	1.5x1 (5x3)	evergreen shrub	white	winter to spring
Cosmos bipinnatus	Cosmos	Asteraceae	0.6x0.5 (2x5)	annual	purple or pink or white	summer to autumn
Cotinus coggygria 'Purpurea'	Smoke bush	Anacardiaceae	5x5 (15x15)	deciduous shrub	mauve	summer to autumn
Cotoneaster horizontalis	Wall-spray	Rosaceae	0.2x1.5 (0.6x5)	deciduous shrub	white	late spring summer
Crataegus x smithiana	Hawthorn	Rosaceae	5x5 (15x15)	semi-deciduous shrub	white	spring
Cuphea llavea 'Tiny Mice'	Cuphea	Lythraceae	0.3x0.5 (1x1.5)	soft-wooded perennial	pink	summer to autumn
Dahlia x hybrida	Dahlia	Asteraceae	0.5-1.2x1 (1.5-4x3)	herbaceous perennial with tuberous roots	all except blue & black	autumn
Daphne odora 'Alba'	Daphne	Thymeleaceae	1.5x1 (5x3)	evergreen shrub	white & purple	winter to spring
Delphinium elatum	Delphinium	Ranunculaceae	1.5-2x0.75 (5-6x2.5)	herbaceous perennial	blue or white	summer to autumn
Dianthus plumarius	Pinks	Caryophyllaceae	0.5x0.3 (1.5x1)	soft-wood perennial	pink, white or purple	spring
Dicksonia antarctica	Soft tree fern	Dicksoniaceae	2-5x3 (6-15x9)	tree fern	n/a	n/a
Digitalis purpurea	Foxgloves	Scrophulariaceae	1-1.5x0.6 (3-5x2)	biennial	pink, white or purple	summer
Dimorphotheca pluvialis	African daisy	Asteraceae	0.3x0.3 (1x1)	annual	white with purple centres	summer
Doryanthes excelsa	Giant spear or Gymea lily	Agavaceae	2-3x3	clumping evergreen perennial	red	spring
Duranta erecta syn *repens*	Pigeon berry	Verbenaceae	2.5x2.5 (8x8)	evergreen shrub	blue	summer
Elaeocarpus reticulatus	Blueberry ash	Elaeocarpaceae	10x3 (30x10)	evergreen shrub	white or pink	spring
Eleagnus pungens 'Maculata'	Eleagnus	Eleagnaceae	4x5 (12x15)	evergreen shrub	cream	autumn
Erigeron karvinskianus (syn. *mucronatus*)	Erigeron	Asteraceae	0.2x2-3 (0.6x6-9)	soft-wood perennial	white ageing to pink & purple	spring to autumn

Colourful features	Preferred climate & growing notes & special uses
flowers & bright red autumn foliage	Cold continental to cool temperate, full sun, good drainage, very frost hardy.
flowers, red fruits, purplish autumn foliage	Cold continental to cool temperate, full sun, good drainage, very frost hardy.
flowers & silvery-green foliage	Warm temperate, full sun, good drainage, mildly frost tolerant. Wonderful for for dune situations in coastal areas.
flowers	Warm temperate to subtropical, full sun, good drainage, mildly frost hardy. Self-seeds readily.
flowers, fruits & purple foliage	Mediterranean to cool temperate, full to part sun, good drainage, very frost hardy. Leaves may be irritating to skin.
flowers & bright red fruits	Cool to warm temperate, full to part sun, good drainage, very frost hardy.
bright red berries & flowers	Cold continental to cool temperate, full sun, good drainage, very frost hardy. There are numerous other attractive Crataegus species and varieties.
flowers	Cool to warm temperate and subtropical, full sun, good drainage, frost tender.
flowers	Cool to warm temperate, full sun, good drainage, mildly frost hardy. Staking of flower stems is desirable for tall varieties. New varieties are available which can be grown from seed.
flowers	Cool to warm temperate, part sun, good drainage, moderately frost hardy, Prefers an acidic soil (pH 5-5.5) and is prone to root rot.
flowers	Cool to warm temperate, full to part sun, good drainage, frost hardy. Needs staking, very prone to powdery mildew.
flowers	Mediterranean to cool temperate, full sun, good drainage, frost hardy. Good cut flower.
foliage & fibrous brown trunk	Cool to warm temperate and subtropical, shaded position, moderate drainage, mildly frost hardy.
flowers	Mediterranean to cool temperate, full sun, good drainage, frost hardy. Needs staking.
flowers	Cool to warm temperate, full sun, good drainage, mildly frost hardy. Self-seeds and forms a good groundcover.
flowers & foliage	Warm temperate, full to part sun, good drainage, mildly frost hardy. Spectacular flowers and bold sword-like leaves.
flowers followed by orange berries in autumn	Warm temperate to subtropical, full sun, good drainage, frost tender.
flowers followed by blue berries	Warm temperate to subtropical , full to part sun, good drainage, frost tender. Flowers have an interesting aniseed perfume. Pink-flowered form is sold as 'Prima Donna'.
flowers & variegated yellow & green leaves	Mediterranean, cool to warm temperate, full sun, good drainage, frost hardy. Flowers are very fragrant.
flowers	Mediterranean, cool to warm temperate., full sun, good drainage, frost hardy. One of the best groundcovering plants available. Provides very low maintenance colour.

Delphinium elatum

Crataegus x smithiana

R. Hyett

Daphne odora

111

Viola x wittrockiana

Black Flowers

*B*lack is perhaps not a colour that we normally associate with flowers but it can provide some very unusual effects in the garden. It is particularly effective when contrasted with white or yellow. Flowers which appear as black are usually the product of very dark purple pigments present in large amounts.

♦ **Black pansies** There are a number of varieties of this ever popular annual which are very close to black. As with most pansies, the black varieties are usually bicolours and the black is set off with a yellow contrast on the petals. Pansies are extremely easy to grow, will reward you with months of flowering at any time of the year, provided there are no frosts. Seedlings will flower several months after planting. They do extremely well in pots or in a well-drained compost enriched garden bed in full sun.

♦ **Black tulips** This is another flower which will draw people towards it in the garden. Once again the colour is actually a very dark purple. Bulbs should be planted in autumn for spring display.

♦ **Black kangaroo paw** (Macropidia fuliginosa) This spectacular flower is actually lime green but is covered in dense black hairs which give it a two-tone appearance. It is a very frustrating plant to grow as it is prone to root rot. It is available as a cut flower and is perhaps best enjoyed this way.

A. Stewart

Botanic name	Common name	Family	Height x width
Eschscholtzia californica	California poppy	Papaveraceae	0.3x0.3m (1x1ft)
Eucalyptus caesia	Gungurru	Myrtaceae	7-10x5 (20-30x15)
Eucalyptus gunnii	Cider gum	Myrtaceae	20x5 (60x15)
Eucalyptus cinerea	Argyle apple	Myrtaceae	20x10 (60x30)
Eucalyptus citriodora	Lemon-scented gum	Myrtaceae	20-30x10-15 (60-90x30-45)
Eucalyptus crenulata	Silver gum	Myrtaceae	10-15x5 (30-45x15)
Eucalyptus pulverulenta	Silver leaved mountain gum	Myrtaceae	5-8x5 (15-25x15)
Euonymus japonicus 'Variegata'	Japanese spindle bush	Celastraceae	3x2 (9x6)
Euphorbia pulcherrima	Poinsettia	Euphorbiaceae	3-4x3 (9-12x9)
Euphorbia wulfenii	Euphorbia	Euphorbiaceae	1x1 (3x3)
Euryops pectinatus	Euryops daisy	Asteraceae	1x1 (3x3)
Felicia amelloides	Kingfisher daisy	Asteraceae	0.3x0.3 (1x1)
Festuca glauca	Blue fescue	Poaceae	0.1x0.1 (0.3x0.3)
Fortunella japonica	Marumi cumquat	Rutaceae	2x1 (6x3)
Fraxinus 'Raywood'	Claret ash	Oleaceae	20x15 (60x45)
Fraxinus excelsior 'Aurea'	Golden ash	Oleaceae	15x8 (45x25)
Freesia x hybrida	Freesia	Iridaceae	0.3x0.3 (1x1)
Gaillardia x grandiflora	Indian blanket	Asteraceae	0.6x0.6 (2x2)
Gardenia augusta	Gardenia	Rubiaceae	1.5x1.5 (5x5)
Gardenia augusta 'Radicans'	Gardenia	Rubiaceae	0.5x1.5 (1.5x5)
Gaura lindheimeri	Butterfly bush	Onagraceae	1.2x0.5 (4x2)
Gazania uniflora	Gazania	Asteraceae	0.2x0.3 (0.6x1)
Ginkgo biloba	Maidenhair tree	Ginkgoaceae	25x5 (75x15)

Plant type	Flower colour	Flowering time	Colourful features	Preferred climate & growing notes & special uses
annual	orange, yellow or white	summer to autumn	flowers	Mediterranean, cool to warm temperate, full sun, good drainage, frost hardy. Self-seeds readily.
evergreen tree	red	winter	flowers & white trunk & branches	Mediterranean to cool temperate, full sun, perfect drainage, frost hardy. Will not perform in humid areas.
evergreen tree	white	summer	flowers & bluish foliage	Cold continental to cool temperate, full sun, good drainage, frost hardy. Foliage good for cut flower arrangements.
evergreen tree	white	summer	flowers & bluish foliage	Mediterranean to cool temperate, full sun, good drainage, frost hardy.
evergreen tree	white	summer	smooth white trunk	Cool to warm temperate, full sun, good drainage, frost hardy. Leaves are strongly lemon-scented.
evergreen tree	white	summer	flowers & bluish foliage	Mediterranean to cool temperate, full sun, moderate drainage, frost hardy.
evergreen tree	white	summer	flowers & bluish foliage	Mediterranean to cool temperate, full sun, good drainage, frost hardy.
evergreen shrub	green	summer	yellow leaf variegation	Mediterranean, cool to warm temperate, full sun, good drainage, frost hardy. Good for coastal areas.
evergreen shrub	red or cream	winter	flowers	Warm temperate to subtropical, full sun, good drainage, frost tender.
evergreen shrub	green	spring	flowers & greyish foliage	Cool to warm temperate, full sun, good drainage, frost hardy.
evergreen shrub	yellow	winter to spring	flowers & greyish foliage	Cool to warm temperate, full sun, good drainage, frost hardy.
evergreen shrub	blue	spring to autumn	flowers	Cool to warm temperate, full sun, good drainage, mildly frost hardy.
evergreen tufting perennial	n/a	n/a	bluish foliage	Mediterranean, cool to warm temperate, full sun, good drainage, frost hardy.
evergreen shrub	white	winter-spring	flowers & small orange fruits	Mediterranean, cool to warm temperate, full sun, good drainage, mildly frost hardy.
deciduous tree	insignificant	n/a	dark red autumn foliage	Mediterranean, cool to warm temperate, full sun, good drainage, very frost hardy.
deciduous tree	insignificant	n/a	bright yellow autumn foliage	Mediterranean, cool to warm temperate, full sun, good drainage, very frost hardy.
corm	various	spring	flowers	Mediterranean, cool to warm temperate, full sun, good drainage, frost hardy.
perennial grown as an annual	orange, red and yellow	summer to autumn	flowers	Mediterranean, cool to warm temperate, full sun, good drainage, very frost hardy. Useful cut flower.
evergreen shrub	white	spring to autumn	flowers & glossy green foliage	Mediterranean, cool to warm temperate, Part sun, good drainage, frost tender. Useful cut flower.
evergreen shrub	white	spring to autumn	flowers & glossy green foliage	Mediterranean, cool to warm temperate, part sun, good drainage, frost tender.
soft-wood perennial	pinkish white	spring to autumn	flowers	Mediterranean, cool to warm temperate, full sun, good drainage, frost hardy.
soft-wood perennial	yellow	spring to autumn	flowers	Mediterranean, cool to warm temperate, full sun, good drainage, mildly frost hardy. Excellent for coastal gardens.
deciduous tree	n/a	n/a	autumn foliage flowers	Mediterranean, cool to warm temperate, full sun, good drainage, very frost hardy.

Botanic name	Common name	Family	Height x width	Plant type	Flower colour	Flowering time
Grevillea robusta	Silky oak	Proteaceae	20x10m (60x30ft)	semi-deciduous tree	gold	spring
Grevillea 'Misty Pink'	'Misty pink' grevillea	Proteaceae	2-3x2 (6-9x6)	evergreen shrub	pink & white	all year
Grevillea 'Robyn Gordon'	'Robyn Gordon' grevillea	Proteaceae	2x3 (6x9)	evergreen shrub	red	all year
Grevillea 'Superb'	'Superb' grevillea	Proteaceae	2x3 (6x9)	evergreen shrub	orange-red	all year
Grevillea juniperina	Juniper-leaved spider flower	Proteaceae	2x3 (6x9)	evergreen shrub	red or yellow	spring to summer
Grevillea victoriae	Royal grevillea	Proteaceae	1.5-2x2 (5-6x6)	evergreen shrub	soft red	autumn to winter
Griselina littoralis 'Variegata'	Griselina	Cornaceae	4x3 (12x9)	evergreen shrub	yellow green	spring
Gypsophila paniculata	Baby's breath	Caryophyllaceae	1.3x2 (4x6)	herbaceous perennial	white	summer
Hamamelis mollis	Witch hazel	Hamamelidaceae	4x4 (12x12)	deciduous shrub	yellow	winter
Hebe speciosa 'La Seduisante'	'La seduisante' hebe	Scrophulariaceae	1x1 (3x3)	evergreen shrub	purple	winter to spring
Hebe x franciscana 'Blue Gem'	'Blue gem' hebe	Scrophulariaceae	0.6x1 (2x3)	evergreen shrub	blue	summer to winter
Hedera helix	Common English Ivy	Araliaceae	depends on support	evergreen climber	green	summer
Helichrysum apiculatum	Everlasting daisy	Asteraceae	0.3x1-2 (1x3-6)	soft-wood perennial	yellow	spring to summer
Helichrysum (syn. *Bracteantha*) *bracteatum*	Everlasting daisy	Asteraceae	1-2x1-2 (3-6x3-6)	soft-wood perennial	all except blue & black	spring to autumn
Helichrysum petiolare 'Limeglow'	Helichrysum	Asteraceae	0.5x1.5 (1.5x4)	evergreen shrub	yellow	summer
Helleborus orientalis	Winter or Lenten rose	Ranunculaceae	0.5x0.5 (1.5x1.5)	herbaceous perennial	white, pink or purple	winter
Hemerocallis varieties	Daylily	Liliaceae	0.5-1.5x1-2 (1.5x5x3-6)	soft-wood perennial	yellow, pink, red, purple & more	summer to autumn
Hibbertia dentata	Trailing guinea flower	Dillenaceae	depends on support	evergreen climber	yellow	spring & summer
Hibbertia scandens	Snake vine	Dillenaceae	depends on support	evergreen climber	yellow	spring & summer
Hyacinthus orientalis	Hyacinth	Liliaceae	0.1-.2x0.1 (0.30.6x0.3)	bulb	pink, white or blue	late winter early spring
Hydrangea macrophylla	Hydrangea	Hydrangeaceae	1.5-2x2 (5-6x6)	deciduous shrub	pink, white or blue	summer
Hymenosporum flavum	Native frangipani	Pittosporaceae	10x5 (30x15)	evergreen tree	yellow	spring

Colourful features	Preferred climate & growing notes & special uses
flowers	Cool to warm temperate and subtropical, full sun, good drainage, mildly frost hardy. Good for attracting birds.
flowers	Warm temperate to subtropical, full sun, good drainage, frost tender. Good for attracting birds.
flowers	Mediterranean, cool to warm temperate, full sun, good drainage, moderately frost hardy. Prune back in late winter. Good for attracting birds.
flowers	Mediterranean, cool to warm temperate, full sun, good drainage, moderately frost hardy. Prune back in late winter. Good for attracting birds.
flowers	Cool to warm temperate, full sun, good drainage, very frost hardy. Good screen plant.
flowers	Cool temperate, full sun, good drainage, very frost hardy. Good screen plant.
yellow variegation on leaves	Cool temperate, full sun, good drainage, frost hardy. Good screen plant. Brightly coloured foliage.
flowers	Mediterranean to cool temperate, full sun, good drainage, frost hardy. Pleasantly perfumed. Great cut flower.
flowers & yellow autumn foliage	Cold continental to cool temperate, full sun, good drainage, very frost hardy. Pleasantly perfumed.
flowers & shiny dark foliage	Cool to warm temperate, full to part sun, good drainage, mildly frost hardy.
flowers & shiny mid green foliage	Cool to warm temperate, full to part sun, good drainage, frost hardy.
various variegated leaf patterns	Cool to warm temperate, full sun to deep shade, moderate drainage, very frost hardy. Many variegated varieties available.
flowers & greyish foliage	Cool to warm temperate, full sun, good drainage, frost hardy. Great groundcover.
flowers	Cool to warm temperate, full sun, good drainage, mildly frost hardy. Best grown as an annual, easily raised from tip cuttings.
flowers & bright foliage	Cool to warm temperate, full sun, good drainage, mildly frost hardy. Great groundcover.
flowers	Cool to warm temperate, part sun to full shade, good drainage, very frost hardy. Great for underplanting around trees.
flowers	Cool to warm temperate, full sun, moderate drainage, frost hardy. Good clumping groundcover.
flowers & bronze green foliage	Warm temperate to subtropical, full to part sun, moderate drainage, frost tender.
flowers	Warm temperate to subtropical, full to part sun, good drainage, frost tender. Good for coastal areas. Great groundcover.
flowers	Cool temperate, full sun, good drainage, frost hardy. Wonderful in pots.
flowers	Cool to warm temperate, full to part sun, good drainage, mildly frost hardy. Prune spent flower heads in winter
flowers & glossy deep green foliage	Warm temperate to subtropical, full sun, good drainage, mildly frost hardy. Beautifully perfumed.

Hydrangea macrophylla

Grevillea robusta

R. Hyett, M. Stoovar

Hyacinthus orientalis

Lavandula stoechas

Impatiens 'New Guinea'

Ixia viridiflora

A. Stewart; D. Harvey

Botanic name	Common name	Family	Height x width
Ilex aquifolium	Holly	Aquifoliaceae	6x4m (18x12ft)
Impatiens walleriana	Busy lizzie	Balsaminaceae	0.5-1x0.5 (2-3x2)
Impatiens New Guinea hybrids	New Guinea hybrid impatiens	Balsaminaceae	0.5-1x0.5 (2-3x2)
Iris x germanica	Bearded iris	Iridaceae	0.6-1.2x0.6 (2-4x2)
Iris pseudacorus	Yellow flag iris	Iridaceae	1-2x0.6 (3-6x2)
Ixia viridiflora	Green ixia	Iridaceae	0.6-1x 0.1 (2-3x0.3)
Jacaranda mimosifolia	Jacaranda	Bignoniaceae	15x10 (45x30)
Jasminum polyanthum	Jasmine	Oleaceae	depends on support
Kerria japonica	Kerria	Rosaceae	2x1.5 (6x5)
Koelreuteria paniculata	Golden rain tree	Sapindaceae	10x10 (30x30)
Lagerstroemia indica	Crepe myrtle	Lythraceae	6-8x5-6 (20-25x15-18)
Lamium galeobdolan (syn. *Galeobdolan argentatum*)	Lamium	Lamiaceae	0.3x indefinite (1x indefinite)
Laurus nobilis	Bay laurel	Lauraceae	10x10 (30x30)
Lavandula angustifolia	English lavender	Lamiaceae	1x0.5 (3x1.5)
Lavandula dentata	French lavender	Lamiaceae	1x0.5 (3x1.5)
Lavandula stoechas	Italian lavender	Lamiaceae	1x0.5 (3x1.5)
Leucadendron argenteum	Silver tree	Proteaceae	6-8x3-4 (20-25x9-12)
Leucadendron laureolum 'Silvan Red'	'Silvan red' leucadendron	Proteaceae	4x2 (12x6)
Liquidambar styraciflua	Liquidambar or Sweetgum	Hamamelidaceae	20-30x10 (60-90x30)
Liriodendron tulipifera	Tulip tree	Magnoliaceae	25x5-8 (75x15-25)
Lobularia maritima	Sweet alyssum	Brassicaceae	0.15x0.3 (0.5x1)
Lomandra longiflora	Spiny mat-rush	Xanthorrhoeaceae	1x1 (3x3)
Lycoris aurea	Golden spider lily	Amaryllidaceae	0.3-0.6x0.1 (1-2x0.3)

116

Plant type	Flower colour	Flowering time	Colourful features	Preferred climate & growing notes & special uses
evergreen shrub	insignificant	spring	glossy dark green leaves & red fruits	Cool temperate, full sun, good drainage, frost hardy. Fruiting may be erratic but mainly grown for foliage.
soft-wood perennial	pink, red, white	all year	flowers	Warm temperate to subtropical, part sun to full shade, frost tender. Self-seeds readily.
soft-wood perennial	all except blue & black	all year	flowers	Warm temperate to subtropical, part sun to full shade, frost tender.
clumping (rhizomatous) perennial	wide variety	spring	flowers & greyish foliage	Mediterranean to cool temperate, full sun, good drainage, frost hardy. Many brilliant colours but over a relatively short flowering season.
clumping (rhizomatous) perennial	yellow	spring	flowers	Mediterranean to cool temperate, full sun, likes bog conditions, frost hardy. Great for poorly drained situations.
perennial corm	green	spring	flowers	Mediterranean, cool to warm temperate, full sun, very good drainage, mildly frost hardy. Very unusual flower colour.
semi-deciduous tree	purple	summer	flowers	Warm temperate to subtropical, full sun, good drainage, mildly frost hardy. One of the world's most beautiful flowering trees.
evergreen climber	pinkish-white	spring	flowers	Warm temperate to subtropical, full to part sun, moderate drainage, frost tender. Can be very invasive if allowed to grow unchecked.
deciduous shrub	yellow	spring	flowers	Cool temperate, full sun, good drainage, frost hardy. Brilliant yellow shrub.
deciduous tree	yellow	summer	flowers & rich yellow autumn foliage	Mediterranean, cool to warm temperate, full sun, good drainage, frost hardy.
deciduous tree	various pastel shades	summer to autumn	flowers, autumn foliage & bark	Mediterranean, cool temperate, full sun, good drainage, mildly frost hardy.
soft-wood perennial	lemon	summer	flowers & foliage	Mediterranean, cool to warm temperate, full sun to deep shade, good drainage, frost hardy.
evergreen tree	yellowish	spring	glossy dark green leaves	Mediterranean, cool to warm temperate, full sun to deep shade, good drainage, frost hardy. Aromatic leaves used for cooking.
evergreen shrub	mauve	late spring to early summer	flowers & grey foliage	Mediterranean to cool temperate, full sun, good drainage, frost hardy. Prune lightly straight after flowering.
evergreen shrub	mauve	winter to spring	flowers & grey foliage	Mediterranean, cool to warm temperate, full sun, good drainage, frost hardy. Prune lightly straight after flowering.
evergreen shrub	purple	late spring to early summer	flowers & grey foliage	Mediterranean, cool to warm temperate, full sun, good drainage, frost hardy. Prune lightly straight after flowering.
evergreen tree	yellowish	spring	foliage has striking silver tones	Mediterranean to cool temperate, full sun good drainage, mildly frost hardy. Foliage can be used in floral arrangements.
evergreen shrub	reddish orange bracts	summer	colour from the bracts which surround the flowers	Mediterranean to cool temperate, full sun good drainage, mildly frost hardy. Flowers and bracts can be used in floral arrangements.
deciduous tree	insignificant	summer	brilliant autumn foliage	Mediterranean, cool to warm temperate, full sun, good drainage, frost hardy. Do not plant near buildings. Varieties such as 'Kia' & 'Tirriki' have been selected for exceptional autumn colour.
deciduous tree	green & orange	spring	flowers & autumn foliage	Mediterranean to cool temperate, full sun, good drainage, deep soil, very frost hardy.
annual	white, purple or pink	summer to autumn	flowers	Mediterranean, cool to warm temperate, full sun, good drainage, frost hardy. Very hardy and self-seeds regularly
soft-wooded rhizomatous perennial	yellow	spring	flowers & bright green strap leaves	Cool to warm temperate, full to part sun, moderate drainage, frost hardy. An excellent foliage plant.
bulb, deciduous	yellow	autumn	flowers & greyish foliage	Warm temperate, full sun, good drainage, frost tender. Good cut flower. Will naturalise readily in warm climates.

Botanic name	Common name	Family	Height x width	Plant type	Flower colour	Flowering time
Lysimachia nummularia 'Aurea'	Creeping Jenny	Primulaceae	0.1mx indefinite (0.3ftx indefinite)	soft wood perennial	yellow	summer
Macropidia fuliginosa	Black kangaroo paw	Haemodoraceae	1.5x0.5 (5x2)	soft wood perennial	green with black hairs	spring
Magnolia denudata	Yulan magnolia	Magnoliaceae	10x10 (30x30)	deciduous tree	white	winter to early spring
Mahonia aquifolium	Oregon grape	Berberidaceae	1-1.5x1.5 (3-5x5)	evergreen shrub	yellow	spring
Matthiola incana	Stock	Brassicaceae	0.5-1x0.3 (1.5-3x1)	annual	white, pink or purple	winter to spring
Melaleuca incana	Grey-leaved honey myrtle	Myrtaceae	2-3x2 (6-9x6)	evergreen shrub	yellow	spring
Michelia figo (syn. *fuscata*)	Port wine magnolia	Magnoliaceae	3x3 (10x10)	evergreen shrub	purple & white	spring
Muscari armenicum	Grape hyacinth	Liliaceae	0.2x0.1 (0.6x0.3)	deciduous bulb	purple	spring
Myosotis sylvatica	Forget-me-not	Boraginaceae	0.3x0.3 (1x1)	perennial grown as an annual	blue	spring
Nandina domestica 'Nana'	Dwarf nandina	Berberidaceae	0.6x0.6 (2x2)	evergreen shrub	white	summer
Narcissus varieties	Jonquil & daffodil	Amaryllidaceae	0.3-1x0.1 (1-3x0.3)	bulb deciduous	white, yellow or pink	winter to spring
Nepeta x faasenii	Catmint	Lamiaceae	0.5x0.5 (1.5x1.5)	soft wood perennial	mauve	summer
Nigella damascena	Love-in-a-mist	Ranunculaceae	0.6x0.3 (2x1)	annual	blue or white	spring
Nyssa sylvatica	Tupelo	Nyssaceae	15x10 (45x30)	deciduous tree	green	summer
Olea europea	European olive	Oleaceae	5x5 (15x15)	evergreen tree	white	summer
Pandorea jasminoides	Bower of beauty	Bignoniaceae	depends on support	evergreen climber	pink or white	spring to summer
Papaver nudicaule	Iceland poppy	Papaveraceae	0.3-0.6x0.3 (1-2x1)	annual	yellow orange pink white	winter spring
Parrotia persica	Ironwood	Hamamelidaceae	10x10 (30x30)	deciduous tree	red	early spring
Perovskia atriplicifolia 'Longin'	Perovskia	Lamiaceae	1x1 (3x3)	soft wood perennial	blue	summer
Persoonia pinifolia	Pine-leaved geebung	Proteaceae	1x2 (3x6)	evergreen shrub	yellow	summer
Petunia x hybrida	Petunia	Solanaceae	0.2-0.3x0.3-1 (0.6-1x1-3)	perennial grown as an annual	blue, purple, red, pink or white or combinations	spring to autumn

Colourful features	Preferred climate & growing notes & special uses
flowers & golden yellow leaves	Mediterranean to cool temperate, full sun, good drainage, very frost hardy. Fantastic groundcover for cooler climates.
flowers & greyish foliage	Mediterranean, full sun, perfect drainage, mildly frost hardy. Difficult to grow, particularly in humid areas.
flowers	Mediterranean to cool temperate, full sun, good drainage, frost hardy. Flowers are sweetly perfumed.
flowers followed by bluish berries	Cool temperate, shady, moderate drainage, very frost hardy.
flowers	Mediterranean, cool to warm temperate, full sun, good drainage, moderately frost hardy. Easily raised from seed sown in autumn. Prefers neutral soil pH.
flowers & soft grey foliage	Mediterranean, cool to warm temperate, full to part sun, moderate drainage, frost hardy. Can be clipped into a formal hedge.
flowers	Warm temperate, full to part sun, good drainage, frost tender.
flowers	Mediterranean to cool temperate, full sun, good drainage, frost hardy. Does not thrive in warmer areas.
flowers	Mediterranean, cool to warm temperate, full to part sun, good drainage, very frost hardy. Self-seeds easily.
reddish foliage all year, intensifying in autumn	Mediterranean, cool to warm temperate, full to part sun, good drainage, very frost hardy.
flowers	Mediterranean, cool to warm temperate, full sun, good drainage, frost hardy. Many varieties available such as 'Erlicheer' or 'Yellow Cheerfulness'. Daffodils may need a cold winter to flower reliably and may not suit warmer climates.
flowers & greyish foliage	Mediterranean, cool to warm temperate, full sun, good drainage, very frost hardy. Foliage has distinctively pleasant aroma. Hardy groundcover.
flowers & seed pods	Mediterranean, cool to warm temperate, full sun, good drainage, very frost hardy.
scarlet to crimson autumn foliage	Cool temperate, full sun, good drainage, frost hardy.
silvery-green foliage, flowers and black fruits	Mediterranean, cool to warm temperate, full sun, good drainage, very frost hardy. Good screen plant. Produces edible fruits.
flowers & glossy green foliage	Warm temperate to subtropical, full sun, good drainage, frost tender. Very long flowering period. Variety 'Lady Di' has beautiful snow-white flowers.
flowers	Cool to warm temperate, full sun, good drainage, frost hardy. Good cut flower.
flowers & yellow, orange & red autumn foliage	Mediterranean to cool temperate, full to part sun, good drainage, very frost hardy. Brilliant multicoloured autumn foliage.
flowers	Mediterranean to cool temperate, full sun, good drainage, very frost hardy. Brilliant blue flower spires.
flowers & purple fruits	Mediterranean, cool to warm temperate, full sun, good drainage, frost hardy. Fruits held in beautiful grape-like clusters. Lovely soft foliage.
flowers	Mediterranean, cool to warm temperate, full sun, good drainage, mildly frost hardy. Extraordinary range of varieties available. Various new varieties are available which cover much larger areas with one plant eg 'Colourwave' varieties.

Petuna x hybrida

Narcissus

R. Hyett; D. Harvey

Nepeta x faasenii

Physostegia virginiana

Picea pungens

Pittosporum tenuifolium

R. Hyett; A. Martin; D. Harvey

Botanic name	Common name	Family	Height x width
Philadelphus coronarius	Mock orange	Hydrangaceae	3x3m (9x9ft)
Phlomis fruticosa	Jerusalem sage	Lamiaceae	0.9x0.9 (3x3)
Phlox drummondii	Annual phlox	Polemoniaceae	0.3x0.2 (1x0.6)
Phlox paniculatus	Perennial phlox	Polemoniaceae	1.2x0.6 (4x2)
Phormium tenax	New Zealand flax plant	Agavaceae	2-3x1-2 (6-9x3-6)
Photinia glabra 'Rubens'	Photinia	Rosaceae	4-5x2 (12-15x6)
Physostegia virginiana	Obedient plant	Lamiaceae	1x0.6 (3x2)
Picea pungens	Colorado blue spruce	Pinaceae	15-20x5 (45-60x15)
Pimelea ferruginea 'Magenta Mist'	Pink rice flower	Thymeleaceae	1x1 (3x3)
Pistacia chinensis	Chinese pistacia	Anacardiaceae	10-15x5-10 (30-45x 15-30)
Pittosporum eugenioides 'Variegatum'	Variegated pittosporum	Pittosporaceae	10x5 (30x15)
Pittosporum tenuifolium 'Irene Patterson'	'Irene Patterson' pittosporum	Pittosporaceae	10x5 (30x15)
Pittosporum tenuifolium 'James Stirling'	'James Stirling' pittosporum	Pittosporaceae	10-14x5 (30-42x15)
Plectranthus oertendahlii	Prostrate plectranthus	Lamiaceae	0.3x2 (1x6)
Plumbago auriculata	Plumbago	Plumbaginaceae	2x3-4 (6x9-12)
Podranea ricasoliana	Pink trumpet vine	Bignoniaeae	depends on support
Polygonatum x hybridum	Solomon's seal	Liliaceae	1x1 (3x3)
Populus nigra 'Italica'	Lombardy poplar	Salicaceae	30-40x5 (90-120x15)
Portulaca grandiflora	Sun plant	Portulacaceae	0.2x0.3 (0.6x1)
Primula malacoides	Primula	Primulaceae	0.3x0.3 (1x1)
Primula obconica	Primula	Primulaceae	0.3x0.3 (1x1)
Prostanthera rotundifolia	Round-leaved mint bush	Lamiaceae	2.5x2 (8x6)
Prunus serrulata	Flowering cherry	Rosaceae-	10x10 (30x30)

Plant type	Flower colour	Flowering time	Colourful features	Preferred climate & growing notes & special uses
deciduous shrub	white	spring	flowers	Mediterranean to cool temperate, full to part sun, good drainage, frost hardy. Delightfully perfumed flowers.
evergreen shrub	yellow	summer	flowers & grey-green foliage	Mediterranean to cool temperate, full sun, good drainage, frost hardy. Brilliant golden-yellow flowers.
annual	cream, pink or red	summer to autumn	flowers	Mediterranean to warm temperate, full sun, good drainage, mildly frost hardy.
soft-wood perennial	cream, pink, violet or red	summer	flowers	Mediterranean to cool temperate, full sun, good drainage, very frost hardy. Forms large clumps. Good cut flower.
soft-wood clumping perennial	bronze-red	summer	flowers & foliage (particularly variegated varieties)	Mediterranean, cool to warm temperate, full sun, moderate drainage frost hardy.Multicoloured foliage can be obtained in varieties, such as 'Sundowner' and 'Rubrum'.
evergreen shrub	white	spring	brilliant red new growth & white flowers	Cool to warm temperate, full sun, good drainage, frost hardy. Prune lightly & regularly during warmer months to encourage red new growth.
herbaceous perennial	mauve or white	summer to autumn	flowers	Mediterranean, cool to warm temperate, full sun, good drainage, very frost hardy. Good cut flower.
evergreen tree	n/a	n/a	glowing blue foliage	Cool temperate to cold continental, full sun good drainage, very frost hardy. Many varieties available in a range of forms and heights.
evergreen shrub	magenta with white centre	spring	flowers & bright glossy foliage	Mediterranean, cool to warm temperate, part sun, good drainage, moderately frost hardy. A very free flowering new variety.
deciduous tree	white	summer	bright red autumn foliage & red fruits	Mediterranean, cool to warm temperate, full sun, moderate drainage, moderately frost hardy. Spectacular autumn foliage.
evergreen tree	yellow	spring	green leaves with white margins	Mediterranean, cool to warm temperate, full sun, good drainage, very frost hardy. An excellent screen plant.
evergreen tree	purple	late spring	greyish variegated foliage	Mediterranean, cool to warm temperate, full sun, good drainage, frost hardy. An excellent screen plant.
evergreen tree	purple	late spring	soft grey-green foliage	Mediterranean, cool to warm temperate, full sun, good drainage, very frost hardy. Makes good cut foliage for flower arrangements.
soft-wood perennial	mauve	all year	flowers & green foliage with purple underside	Warm temperate to subtropical, part sun, good drainage, frost tender. An excellent groundcover beneath trees & shrubs in warmer climates. Easily propagated.
evergreen shrub	blue or white	summer to autumn	flowers	Warm temperate to subtropical, full sun, good drainage, frost tender. Suckers from the base, can be pruned very hard after flowering.
evergreen climber	pink	spring to autumn	flowers	Warm temperate to subtropical, full sun, good drainage, frost tender. Brilliant long flowering but rampant climber.
rhizomatous perennial	white	spring	flowers	Cool temperate, full shade, good drainage, very frost hardy. Great plant for very shady situations in cool climates.
deciduous tree	insignificant	spring	yellow autumn foliage	Mediterranean, cool to warm temperate, full sun, good drainage, very frost hardy. Unusual column-shaped tree. Suckers from roots and is only suitable for very large gardens.
annual	pink, red or yellow	summer to autumn	brightly coloured flowers	Warm temperate to subtropical, full sun, good drainage, frost tender. Fast growing annual for a bright mixture of colours.
perennial grown as an annual	pink, purple or white	spring	flowers	Warm temperate, part sun, good drainage, frost tender. Beautiful candelabra-shaped flower heads.
soft-wood perennial	pink, purple or white	winter to spring	flowers	Warm temperate, part sun, good drainage, frost tender. Beautiful candelabra-shaped flower heads.
evergreen shrub	mauve	spring	flowers	Warm temperate, part sun, perfect drainage, mildly frost hardy. Wonderfully perfumed foliage.
deciduous tree	white	spring	flowers, autumn foliage & red bark	Mediterranean to cool temperate, full sun, good drainage, very frost hardy. An outstanding ornamental tree for cooler climates with several beautiful features.

Botanic name	Common name	Family	Height x width	Plant type	Flower colour	Flowering time
Prunus x blireana	Prunus	Rosaceae	3.5-5x3-4m (10-15x 9-12ft)	deciduous tree	pink	spring
Pyracantha fortuneana	Firethorn	Rosaceae	3x4 (9x12)	evergreen shrub	white	spring
Pyrostegia venusta	Flame vine	Bignoniaceae	depends on support	evergreen tendril climber	orange	autumn to winter & spring
Quercus coccinea	Scarlet oak	Fagaceae	20x10 (60x30)	deciduous tree	yellowish-green	spring
Quercus palustris	Pin oak	Fagaceae	20x10 (60x30)	deciduous tree	yellowish-green	spring
Ranunculus asiaticus	Ranunculus	Ranunculaceae	0.6x0.1 (2x0.3)	perennial tuber	all except blue &black	spring
Raphiolepis indica	Indian hawthorn	Rosaceae	2x2 (6x6)	evergreen shrub	white	spring
Raphiolepis x delacourii	Pink Indian hawthorn	Rosaceae	2x2 (6x6)	evergreen shrub	pink	spring
Rhagodia spinescens	Spiny saltbush	Chenopodiaceae	0.6 x1.5 (2x5)	evergreen ground covering shrub	greenish	summer
Rhododendron species & varieties	Large-leaved rhododendron	Ericaceae	2-10x2-4 (6-30x6-12)	evergreen shrub	all except blue & black	winter to spring
Rhododendron (syn. Azalea) varieties	Azalea	Ericaceae	2-5x2-4 6-15x6-12	evergreen or deciduous	all except blue & black	autumn to spring
Robinia pseudoacacia 'Frisia'	False acacia or black locust	Fabaceae	20x10 (60x30)	deciduous tree	white	spring
Rosa 'Carabella'	Carabella rose	Rosaceae	2x2 (6x6)	deciduous shrub	cream or pink with yellow centre	spring to autumn
Rosa 'Cecile Brunner'	Sweetheart rose	Rosaceae	2x2 (6x6)	deciduous shrub	pink double flowers	spring to autumn
Rosa 'Iceberg'	Iceberg rose	Rosaceae	1x1 (3x3)	deciduous shrub	white double flowers	spring to autumn
Rosa banksiae	Banksia rose	Rosaceae	8x8 (25x25)	deciduous climber	white single flowers	spring
Rudbeckia fulgida	Coneflower	Asteracea	1x1 (3x3)	soft-wood perrenial	yellow with black centre	summer to autumn
Salix babylonica	Weeping willow	Salicaceae	20x20 (60x60)	decidious tree	yellowish	spring
Salvia splendens	Red salvia	Lamiaceae	0.3x0.3 (1x1)	perennial grown as an annual	red	summer to autumn
Sapium sebiferum	Chinese tallow tree	Euphorbiaceae	10x5 (30x15)	deciduous tree	greenish-yellow	summer
Scabiosa 'Butterfly Blue'	'Butterfly blue' scabious	Dipsacaceae	0.6x0.6 (2x2)	soft wood perennial	blue	summer to autumn
Schefflera actinophylla	Umbrella tree	Araliaceae	6-8x3 (18-25x10)	evergreen tree	crimson	summer to autumn
Schinus areira	Peppercorn tree	Anacardiaceae	10-15x10 (30-45x30)	evergreen tree	white	spring to summer

Colourful features	Preferred climate & growing notes & special uses
flowers & beautiful dark red foliage	Mediterranean, cool to warm temperate, full sun, good drainage, very frost hardy. Leaves retain their dark red colour right through the growing season.
scarlet fruits in autumn and flowers	Mediterranean, cool to warm temperate, full sun, good drainage, frost hardy. The fruits make a long lasting display through autumn and winter.
flowers	Warm temperate to subtropical, full sun, good drainage, frost tender. A very spectacular climber at its peak in winter.
scarlet autumn foliage	Mediterranean to cool warm temperate, full sun, good drainage, very frost hardy. Autumn colour remains on the tree for a month or so.
red autumn foliage	Mediterranean to cool temperate, full sun, good drainage, very frost hardy. A fast growing species of oak.
flowers	Mediterranean, cool to warm temperate, full sun, good drainage, frost hardy.
flowers & black berries	Mediterranean, cool to warm temperate, full sun, good drainage, frost hardy. Berries last a long time on the bush in winter to add interest. Flowers are fragrant.
flowers & bluish berries	Mediterranean, cool to warm temperate, full sun, good drainage, moderately frost hardy. Berries last a long time on the bush in winter to add interest. Flowers are fragrant.
greyish foliage & red fruits	Mediterranean, to cool temperate, full sun, good drainage, frost hardy. A useful drought-tolerant groundcover.
flowers	Mediterranean to cool temperate, part sun, good drainage, frost hardy. Numerous varieties.
flowers	Mediterranean, cool to warm temperate, full to part sun, good drainage, most varieties frost hardy. Numerous varieties
yellow foliage through entire growing season	Mediterranean, cool to warm temperate, full sun, good drainage, frost hardy. A brilliant foliage tree over a wide range of climates.
flowers	Mediterranean, cool to warm temperate, full sun, good drainage, frost hardy. Fragrant and long flowering cluster-flowered rose.
flowers	Mediterranean, cool to warm temperate, full sun, good drainage, frost hardy. There is also a climbing type of this variety available.
flowers	Mediterranean, cool to warm temperate, full sun, good drainage, very frost hardy. One of the best white varieties available for a range of climates.
flowers	Mediterranean, cool to warm temperate, full sun, good drainage, frost hardy. A very hardy rampant climbing rose.
flowers	Mediterranean, cool to warm temperate, full to part sun, good drainage, frost hardy. Unusual flowers are good for cutting.
yellow autumn foliage	Mediterranean, cool to warm temperate, full sun, poor drainage, frost hardy.
flowers	Mediterranean, cool to warm temperate, full sun, good drainage, mildly frost hardy. Spectacular red display, easily raised from seed to flower in a season.
multicoloured autumn foliage	Mediterranean, cool to warm temperate, full sun, good drainage, moderately frost hardy.
flowers	Mediterranean, cool to warm temperate, full sun, good drainage, frost hardy. Excellent long flowering perennial.
flowers & reddish fruits	Warm temperate to subtropical, full to part sun, good drainage, frost tender. Spectacular in flower, attracts birds. Commonly used as an indoor plant.
flowers & masses red-pink fruits	Mediterranean, cool to warm temperate, full sun, good drainage, moderately frost hardy. Aromatic foliage & fruits. Attractive weeping habit. Drought tolerant.

Rudbeckia

Rosa 'Iceberg'

Salvia splendens

D. Brice; D. Harvey

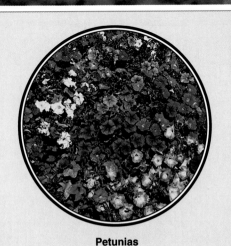

Petunias

Public Plantings

*I*f your garden is to be a restful retreat, a place of solace from the pressures of day to day living, and a place to recharge your batteries, green, grey and white plants and flowers will probably play a major role.

However, beyond your garden in the public spaces of shopping and commercial centres, railway stations, civic areas and parks, vibrant plantings and daring colour combinations can be quite exhilarating. Colour schemes of which we would quickly tire if we were surrounded by them every day, become tonics. They work well because of their situation and our limited exposure to them but when transported to our home gardens, these plantings are rarely successful.

Memorable garden schemes are usually simple ones in which just a few colours are used; variety and interest are provided by different plant shapes and textures. Monochromatic plantings can be very successful as they provide an effective focus and overall harmony. Maintain some colour in your garden throughout the year by choosing plants which flower at different times, and feature colours that complement your existing scheme.

Botanic name	Common name	Family	Height x width
Scleranthus biflorus	Scleranthus	Caryophyllaceae	0.1x0.6m (0.3x2ft)
Sedum spectabile	Sedum	Crassulaceae	0.6x0.6 (2x2)
Senecio cineraria	Dusty miller	Asteraceae	1x0.6 (3x2)
Sparaxis tricolor	Harlequin flower	Iridaceae	0.3x0.1 (1x0.3)
Stachys byzantina	Lamb's ears	Lamiaceae	0.6x0.6 (2x2)
Stenocarpus sinuatus	Firewheel tree	Proteaceae	10-15x5 (30-45x15)
Syzigium australe	Scrub cherry	Myrtaceae	5-8x5 (15-24x15)
Syzigium paniculatum	Brush cherry	Myrtaceae	20x8 (60x25)
Tagetes erecta 'Moonbeam' & 'Solar Gold'	African marigold	Asteraceae	1x0.3 (3x1)
Trachelospermum jasminoides	Star jasmine	Apocynaceae	depends on support
Tropaeolum majus 'Mutabilis'	Nasturtium	Tropaeolaceae	0.3x0.6 (1x2)
Tulipa x hybrida	Tulip	Liliaceae	0.3-0.6x0.2 (1-2x0.6)
Viola tricolor	Heartsease	Violaceae	0.15x0.15 (0.5x0.5)
Viola hederacea	Australian native violet	Violaceae	0.1x 1 (0.3x3)
Viola x wittrockiana	Pansy	Violaceae	0.2x.0.2 (0.5x0.5)
Virgilia oroboides	Tree in a hurry	Fabaceae	8x5 (25x15)
Vitex trifolia	Vitex	Verbenaceae	2-3x3 (6-9x9)
Westringia longifolia	Westringia	Lamiaceae	2x1 (6x3)
Wisteria sinensis	Wisteria	Fabaceae	depends on support
Yucca aloifolia	Spanish bayonet	Agavaceae	2x2 (6x6)
Zantedischia aethiopica	White arum lily	Araceae	0.5-1x0.5 (2-3x2)
Zantedischia aethiopica 'Green Goddess'	Green arum lily	Araceae	0.5-1x0.5 (2-3x2)
Zephyranthes candida	Rain lily	Amaryllidaceae	0.25x0.1 (1x0.3)

Plant type	Flower colour	Flowering time	Colourful features	Preferred climate & growing notes & special uses
soft-wood clumping perennial	white	spring	bright green foliage	Mediterranean to cool temperate, full sun, good drainage, frost hardy. An interesting alternative groundcover to lawns.
soft-wood perennial (succulent)	pink	summer	flowers & grey-green foliage	Mediterranean, cool to warm temperate, full sun, good drainage, very frost hardy. Drought tolerant and will thrive in coastal conditions. Nice foliage plant.
soft-wood perennial	yellow	summer	flowers & silvery-grey foliage	Mediterranean, cool to warm temperate, full sun, good drainage, very frost hardy. Good for exposed positions, drought tolerant. Wonderful foliage plant.
perennial corm	orange, red or pink with black & yellow centre	spring	flowers	Mediterranean to warm temperate, full sun, good drainage, mildly frost hardy. Stunning multi-coloured flowers.
soft-wood perennial	mauve	summer	flowers & silver foliage	Mediterranean, cool to warm temperate, full sun, good drainage, very frost hardy. Stunning contrast plant. Drought tolerant.
evergreen tree	red	summer	flowers & glossy green foliage	Warm temperate to subtropical, full sun, good drainage, frost tender. Spectacular in flower and attracts birds.
evergreen shrub to small tree	white	summer	flowers & bright red fruits	Warm temperate to subtropical, full to part sun, good drainage, frost tender. Fruits are edible. Great screen plant, compact varieties available.
evergreen small tree	white	summer	flowers & crimson fruits & red new growth	Warm temperate to subtropical, full to part sun, good drainage, frost tender. Fruits are edible. Great screen plant, compact varieties available.
annual	yellow or orange	summer to autumn	flowers	Mediterranean, cool to warm temperate, full sun, good drainage, moderately frost hardy. Deadhead regularly for longer flowering.
evergreen climber	white	summer	flowers & shiny green foliage	Mediterranean to warm temperate, full sun, good drainage, moderately frost hardy. Beautifully perfumed flowers. Can also be used as a spreading groundcover.
annual	orange, red or yellow	summer to autumn	flowers & variegated foliage	Mediterranean, cool to warm temperate, full sun, good drainage, frost hardy. Fast growing annual capable of providing quick groundcover. Edible flowers.
perennial bulb	all except blue	spring	flowers & greyish foliage	Mediterranean to cool temperate, full sun, good drainage, frost hardy. Excellent potted plants. Difficult to reflower in warmer climates.
annual	purple & yellow	spring to autumn	flowers	Mediterranean, cool to warm temperate, full sun, good drainage, very frost hardy. Self-seeds readily and has perfumed flowers.
soft-wood perennial	purple & white	spring to autumn	flowers	Mediterranean to warm temperate, shady situation, good drainage, mildly frost hardy. Fantastic groundcover for shady conditions.
annual	various	all year	flowers	Mediterranean, cool to warm temperate, full to part sun, good drainage, very frost hardy. Many different varieties including black ones.
evergreen tree	pink	spring to autumn	flowers	Mediterranean, cool to warm temperate, full sun, good drainage, frost hardy. Very quick grower to provide a medium term screen.
evergreen shrub	mauve	summer to autumn	flowers & purplish foliage	Warm temperate, full sun, good drainage, frost tender. Wonderful spreading foliage plant.
evergreen shrub	pale blue	spring to summer	flowers	Mediterranean, cool to warm temperate, full sun, good drainage, frost hardy.
deciduous climber	purple	spring	flowers & velvet green seed pods	Mediterranean, cool to warm temperate, full to part sun, good drainage, frost hardy. A rampant but very beautiful climber.
evergreen shrub	white	summer to autumn	flowers & greyish foliage	Warm temperate, full sun, good drainage, frost tender. Dramatic appearance with tufts of sword-like greyish leaves.
soft wooded perennial	white	spring to summer	flowers	Mediterranean, cool to warm temperate, shady situation, bogy conditions, frost hardy. Great for shady swampy spots in the garden. Very hardy and long-lived.
soft wooded perennial	white with green tips	spring to summer	flowers	Mediterranean, cool to warm temperate, shady situation, bogy conditions, frost hardy. Great for shady swampy spots in the garden. Unusual flower colour.
perennial bulb	white	autumn	flowers & glossy green grass-like foliage	Mediterranean, cool to warm temperate, full to part sun, moderate drainage, frost hardy.

Index

World Climate Zones

Use this map to locate areas of the world with a climate similar to your own. Plants from those regions are most likely to be successful in your garden. Plants that suit your climate will thrive while those from a different zone may need coddling and special treatment to survive.

KEY TO MAP

Tundra: Average summer temperature 0-10°C (32-50°F). Very severe winters.

Sub-Arctic: Severe winters. Average temperature above 10°C (50°F) for less than four months.

Cold continental: Rain year-round or dry winters. Average summer temperatures below 22°C (72°F).

Cool continental: Severe winters but warm to hot summers. May be rainy year-round or dry in winter.

Temperate: Cool winters, warm summers. May be rainy year-round or wet in winter.

Subtropical: Cool to mild winters, warm to hot summers. May be rainy year-round or dry in winter.

Mediterranean: Cool to mild winters, warm to hot summers. Summers always dry.

Semi-arid plains: Relatively low rainfall which may be seasonal or evenly spread. Cold, cool or mild winters.

Desert: Very low rainfall. Winters may be cold or mild.

Tropical: Year-round warmth above 18°C (64°F). High rainfall, heaviest in summer; winters may be dry or less wet.

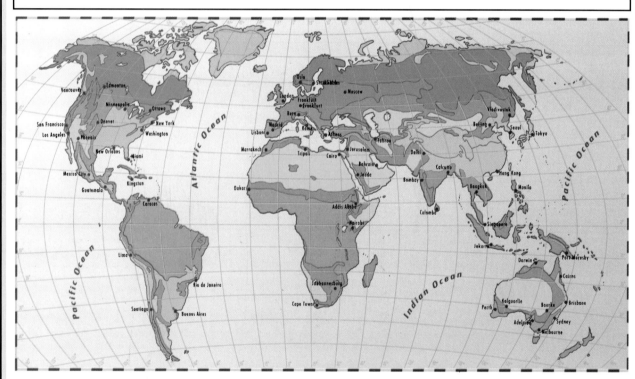

Our terms defined:

RAIN:
Includes snowfalls.

COLD:
Where average temperatures in winter are always below 0°C (32°F).

COOL:
Where average temperatures in winter are between 0°-7°C (32°- 45°F).

MILD:
Where average temperatures in winter are above 0°-7°C (32°F).

WARM:
Where average temperatures in summer are below 20°C (68°F).

HOT:
Where average temperatures in summer are above 20°C (68°F).

Richard de Waal